MW00789263

Sanctum of Shadows

Volume II

Corpus Satanas

Aleister Nacht

SANCTUM OF SHADOWS CORPUS SATANAS

© 2014 ALEISTER NACHT

PUBLISHED BY LOKI/SPECKBOHNE PUBLISHING

NO PART OF THIS BOOK MAY BE REPRODUCED
BY ANY MEANS WITHOUT PRIOR WRITTEN
PERMISSION OF THE BOOK PUBLISHER.

ALL RIGHTS RESERVED

ISBN-10: 0985707097

ISBN-13: 978-0-9857070-9-5

FIRST EDITION PRINT

10 9 8 7 6 5 4 3 2 1

PRINTED IN THE UNITED STATES OF AMERICA

SANCTUM OF SHADOWS CORPUS SATANAS

CONNECT WITH ALEISTER NACHT

Website

www.AleisterNacht.com

Satanic Magic Blog

www.SatanicMagic.Wordpress.com

Facebook

www.Facebook.com/Aleister.Nacht

Twitter

www.Twitter.com/AleisterNacht

The Coven

www.AleisterNacht.podbean.com

Publisher

www.LokiSpeckbohne.com

"THERE IS THE LEGEND OF EVE AND THE SER-
PENT, FOR CAIN WAS THE CHILD OF EVE AND THE
SERPENT, AND NOT OF EVE AND ADAM; AND
THEREFORE WHEN HE HAD SLAIN HIS BROTHER, WHO
WAS THE FIRST MURDERER, HAVING SACRIFICED
LIVING THINGS TO HIS DEMON, HAD CAIN THE
MARK UPON HIS BROW, WHICH IS THE MARK OF
THE BEAST SPOKEN OF IN THE APOCALYPSE, AND IS
THE SIGN OF INITIATION."

THE BOOK OF THOTH
ALEISTER CROWLEY

"PARCUS DEORUM CULTOR, ET INFREQUENS,
INSANIENTIS DUM SAPIENTIÆ CONSULTUS ERRO;
NUNC RETRORSUM VELA DARE, ATQUE ITERARE
CURSUS COGOR RELICTOS"

QUINTUS HORATIUS FLACCUS
(HORACE)

Nomina Actorum

"YOU WANT IT ALL
BUT YOU CAN'T HAVE IT
IT'S IN YOUR FACE
BUT YOU CAN'T GRAB IT

WHAT IS IT?"[1]

---

[1] *Faith No More - "Epic"*

PART I - FUNDAMENTA INCONCUSSA

PRAELUDIUM

I. SATAN, WE CALL UPON YOU AND YOUR LE-
GION OF DEMONS TO OPEN THE DOOR OF TRUTH
AND KNOWLEDGE. WE ARE YOUR SATANIC
ACOLYTES.

II. WE <u>HUMBLY</u> ASK FOR YOUR BLESSINGS AND
ASK <u>BOLDLY</u> FOR YOUR ASSISTANCE AS WE KNOW
YOU REVEAL THE TRUTH. YOU WANT US TO KNOW
THE TRUTH!

III. FAR TOO LONG HAS HUMANITY WALKED
IN DARKNESS, ENDURING LIES AND DECEPTION OF
THOSE WHO WISH TO REND OUR FLESH AND TEAR US
FROM LIMB.

IV. WE UNDERSTAND YOUR DEMONS REVEAL
THE TRUTH AS WE DELVE INTO THE WORLD OF SA-
TANIC MAGIC.

V. WE ARE SINCERE, HONEST AND FORTHRIGHT
SATANISTS SEEKING TRUTH IN THE PERSONIFICA-
TION OF YOU.

VI. LET EVIL RAIN UPON THE EARTH UNDER THE CANOPY OF THE SKY, FOR THIS WE CALL UPON THE LEGIONS. GRANT OUR DESIRES AND SATISFY OUR HUNGER FOR KNOWLEDGE.

VII. SATAN, LEVIATHAN, AZAZEL, SAMAEL! HEAR OUR VOICES. BALAN, RÄUM, CAYM, PERCHTA, ZEPAR, FÜTGLE! WE CALL UPON THE DEMONS OF HELL!

VIII. WE DEDICATE OUR MINDS, ACTIONS AND BODIES TO YOU SATAN; FROM YOU WE GAIN INFINITE KNOWLEDGE AND WISDOM IN OUR SATANIC ORDER.

IX. HAIL SATAN! HAIL LEVIATHAN! HAIL AZAZEL! HAIL SAMAEL! HAIL BALAN! HAIL RÄUM! HAIL CAYM! HAIL PERCHTA! HAIL ZEPAR! HAIL FÜTGLE!

X. EMPOWER THIS WORK AND BLESS THOSE WHO READ ITS WORDS SO THEY MAY UNDERSTAND AND EXPERIENCE WHAT IS BEYOND REASON. SO IT SHALL BE!

ET CUM SPIRITU TUO

"THERE ARE DIFFERENT ORDERS (ORDNUNG) OF DEMONS. A WORKING KNOWLEDGE OF THE HIERARCHY IS IMPORTANT AND YOU MUST INVEST TIME FOR AN UNDERSTANDING.

WHEN A DEMON FIRST APPEARS, IT WILL BE A SHOCKING AND BAFFLING EXPERIENCE. EVERYTHING YOU HAVE BEEN TAUGHT TO BELIEVE AND HAVE ACCEPTED AS THE TRUTH IS SUDDENLY CALLED INTO QUESTION; YOUR BELIEF SYSTEM WILL BE TURNED UPSIDE DOWN."[2]

ALEISTER NACHT

SATAN (HEBREW: הַשָּׂטָן HA-SATAN, "THE AC-CUSER", ARABIC: "SHAITAN") - IS WIDELY KNOWN AS A CHARACTER APPEARING IN THE TEXTS OF THE ABRAHAMIC RELIGIONS, WHO PERSONIFIES EVIL AND TEMPTATION, AND IS KNOWN AS THE DECEIV-ER.

THE TERM IS OFTEN APPLIED TO THE DEVIL WHO

---

[2] *"How to Summon Satanic Demons"* by Aleister Nacht (http://goarticles.com/article/How-to-Summon-Satanic-Demons/5607319/)

FELL OUT OF HEAVENLY FAVOR, SEDUCING HU-
MANITY INTO THE WAYS OF SIN, AND WHO NOW
RULES OVER THIS FALLEN WORLD.

FOR THEISTIC SATANISTS, SATAN IS POSITIVE
FORCE AND A DEITY TO BE WORSHIPPED AND
REVERED; SATAN IS LOVE AND BEAUTY. THE ESTAB-
LISHED MODERN RELIGIONS OF TODAY HAVE BAS-
TARDIZE SATAN; THEY HAVE TURNED HIM INTO A
VILLAIN AS OPPOSED TO WHAT HE TRULY IS; "THE
BRINGER OF LIGHT AND TRUTH".

IT IS UNEQUIVOCALLY TRUE THAT SATAN KEEPS
THE XTIAN CHURCH (AS WELL AS OTHER RELIGIONS)
IN BUSINESS. SATAN HOWEVER, HAS BEEN AND
ALWAYS WILL BE HUMANITY'S BEST FRIEND. HE
HAS ALWAYS COMMUNICATED TRUTH TO
MANKIND AND PROVIDED GENTLE DIRECTION FOR
MAKING THE DIFFICULT CHOICES IN HUMAN LIFE.
SATAN IS MORE CONCERNED WITH THE HUMAN'S
WELL-BEING THAT THE SUPPOSEDLY "LOVING" GODS
AND MESSIAHS OF THE ESTABLISHED LEGACY RELI-
GIONS. SATAN HAS ALWAYS SPOKEN THE TRUTH
WHILE THE IGNORANT AND SIMPLE-MINDED
DROWNED OUT HIS 'LONE VOICE IN THE WILDER-
NESS'.

RELIGIONS TODAY REMAIN AT ODDS WITH THE TRUTH OF SATAN; NO ONE HAS BEEN MORE OF AN ADVOCATE FOR THE HUMAN RACE THAN SATAN HIMSELF. AS THE SAYING GOES "IN GOD THEY TRUST, IN SATAN THEY FEAR".

THROUGHOUT THE AGES, SATAN HAS BEEN BRANDED AN EVIL PRESENCE AND A BEING HUMANS CANNOT TRUST. IN MUCH OF THEIR DOCUMENTATION ABOUT SATAN, HE IS OFTEN PORTRAYED AS A SERPENT; ONE WHO IS CONSTANTLY NEGOTIATING WITH HUMANS IN ORDER TO STEAL THEIR SOULS; THIS IS NOT TRUE REALITY.

SATAN IS THE BEST FRIEND HUMANS HAVE EVER HAD. HE TELLS THE TRUTH; NEITHER SPEAKING LIES NOR DOES HE REQUIRE HUMAN SLAVERY TO ACHIEVE HIS KINGDOM AS THE OTHER SO-CALLED "GODS" MENTIONED IN ESTABLISH RELIGIOUS LITERATURE. EVEN THE CHURCH THAT ADOPTED HIS NAME HAS BEEN AT ODDS WITH THE IDEA OF HIS VERY EXISTENCE. HUMANITY WOULD RATHER BELIEVE A LIE THAN THE TRUTH.

"THE CHURCH OF SATAN AVOIDED THIS PARADOX BY THE SIMPLE TECHNIQUE OF REFUSING TO

CONFRONT IT DIRECTLY. AN ATMOSPHERE OF PSY-
CHODRAMATIC ATHEISM PREVAILED. SATAN WAS
CEREMONIALLY INVOKED WITH GREAT FERVOR,
BUT IN NON-CEREMONIAL SURROUNDINGS EVEN
THE MOST DIE-HARD SATANISTS HESITATED TO TAKE
A POSITION CONCERNING HIS REALITY. IF REFER-
ENCES TO HIS EXISTENCE WERE MADE, THEY WERE
VAGUE, CAUTIOUS, AND HYPOTHETICAL."[3]

I HAVE BEEN GREATLY, SATANICALLY BLESSED
WITH THE KNOWLEDGE THAT IS SHARED IN THIS
BOOK (AS WELL AS MY OTHER BOOKS). SATAN CON-
TINUES TO BLESS ME WITH THE WORDS HE WANTS
TO BE WRITTEN AND I AM ONLY A WILLING IN-
STRUMENT OF HIS COMMUNICATION FROM BE-
YOND THE PARALLAX DIMENSION[4].

I HAVE WRITTEN AT GREAT LENGTH ABOUT SA-
TAN, AS HE IS THE VERY FOUNDATION OF OUR
COVEN'S SYSTEM OF BELIEF[5]; CONTINUING TO IN-
SPIRE, BLESS, DIRECT AND REWARD OUR DILIGENT
WORK IN HIS NAME.

---

[3] *Black Magic* by Michael A. Aquino

[4] Also called the *Paradox Dimension* http://satanicmagic.wordpress.com/2013/09/20/halloween-satanism-and-esprit-de-corps/

[5] Magnum Opus Satanic Coven *http://satanicmagic.wordpress.com/about/*

IT IS BY HIS AUTHORITY THAT I HAVE RISEN THROUGH THE RANKS TO HOLD THE SACRED OFFICE OF MAGUS IN HIS SATANIC INSTITUTION. FOR THAT, I AM ETERNALLY THANKFUL AND AC-KNOWLEDGEABLE HOWEVER, THIS BOOK IS ABOUT THOSE SATANIC DEMONS WHO ARE THE "FOOT SOL-DIERS" OF HIS MAJESTIC KINGDOM. WITHOUT THESE ABLE BEINGS, THE CONNECTION WITH SATAN AND THE WILL OF SATANIC MAGIC WOULD CER-TAINLY BE MOST DIFFICULT IF NOT, IMPOSSIBLE.

A DEMON (AKA DAEMON OR FIEND) IS A SU-PERNATURAL, OFTEN MALEVOLENT BEING PREVA-LENT IN RELIGION, OCCULTISM, LITERATURE, FIC-TION, MYTHOLOGY AND FOLKLORE. THE ORIGINAL GREEK WORD "DAIMON" DOES NOT CARRY THE NEGATIVE CONNOTATION INITIALLY UNDERSTOOD. DEMONOLOGY IS THE STUDY OF DEMONS AND DEMONIC FORCES. THERE ARE XTIAN, JEWISH, IS-LAMIC, OCCULT AND ZOROASTRIAN DEMONOLO-GISTS WHO FOCUS ON TYPES OF DEMONS, HISTORY, LORE AND MODERN DEMONIC ACTIVITY. THE WORD NETER HAS BEEN TRANSLATED "GOD-LIKE", "HOLY", "DIVINE", "SACRED", "POWER", "STRENGTH", "FORCE", "STRONG", "FORTIFY",

"MIGHTY" AND "PROTECT".[6] THE NETER OF THE SATANIC DEMON IS CERTAINLY HIS / HER ABILITY TO PERFORM THOSE TASKS THAT REMAIN BEYOND THE HUMAN'S GRASP AND IN SOME CASES, COGNITIVE ABILITY. THE SATANIC DEMON IS ABLE TO PEER INTO THE INTENSION AND DESIRE OF THE PRACTITIONER AND "FILL THE GAPS"; THUS BRIDGING THE CHASM; METAPHORICALLY SMOOTHING THE 'ROCKY' TERRAIN OF MAGICAL PRACTICE AND OPERATIONS.

ALCHEMY AND SATANIC MAGIC GO HAND IN HAND. IN ORDER TO PREPARE A POTION OR ANY OTHER COMPOSITION AS NEEDED BY THE MAGIC PRACTITIONER, YOU MUST HAVE A GRASP OF ALCHEMY. BLENDING SUBSTANCES TOGETHER AND INJECTING A LARGE DOSE OF MAGIC IS AT THE VERY HEART OF A MAGICAL OPERATION AND MORE SPECIFICALLY, THE HIGHER SATANIC PROCESSES. AS I PROVIDE GUIDANCE AND KNOWLEDGE IN THIS BOOK, I WILL ALSO INCLUDE SOME INFORMATION YOU MAY FIND USEFUL TO YOUR PRACTICE OF MAGIC.

IF YOU ARE ABLE TO LIGHT AND EXTINGUISH A

---

[6] *Black Magic* by Michael A. Aquino

CANDLE FROM A DISTANCE, YOU KNOW IT IS A MAGICAL PROCESS; A TANGIBLE PROCESS THAT RESULTS ALMOST INSTANTANEOUSLY. THE HIGHER SATANIC PROCESSES OF MAGIC WORK IN A SIMILAR FASHION HOWEVER, IT MAY TAKE MORE THAN AN HOUR OR TWO PER WEEK IN ORDER TO REALIZE TRUE SUCCESS.

YOU MUST, AS A PRACTITIONER, HAVE PATIENCE WHILE DILIGENTLY PURSUING PERFECTION. YOU WILL CERTAINLY PRACTICE MANY, MANY HOURS AND EXPEND MASSIVE AMOUNTS OF ENERGY, ONLY TO FAIL TIME AFTER TIME. LET ME SAY THIS; "YOU WILL NEVER TRULY FAIL IF YOU ARE APPLYING THE KNOWLEDGE AND DILIGENTLY, SINCERELY SEEKING SUCCESS AND PERFECTION".

JUST AS MAGIC IS BASED UPON PROCESSES, LEARNING ALSO REQUIRES THE APPLICATION OF PROCESSES. YOU WILL BE ACQUIRING NEW SKILLS AND DILIGENTLY WORKING TO PERFECT THOSE NEW SKILLS (INCLUDING INABILITY TO ACHIEVE THE DESIRED RESULT) IS REQUIRED.

THERE IS NO SUCH THING AS "FAILURE" WHEN IT COMES TO THESE MAGICAL PROCESSES. YOU MUST INVEST THE TIME BUT EVERYTHING YOU ARE

LEARNING IS A DIRECT PRODUCT OF YOUR MAGICAL "EQUATIONS". YOU MUST LEARN THOSE THINGS THAT WORK AND THOSE THINGS THAT DO NOT WORK. IT DOES NOT MEAN THAT YOU ARE FAILING IN YOUR ENDEAVOR; IT SIMPLY MEANS YOU ARE, AS ALL GREAT PRACTITIONERS OF MAGIC, EXPERIMENTING IN ORDER TO FIND THAT WHICH CONSISTENTLY PRODUCES YOUR DESIRES.

AS AN ALCHEMIST, YOU WILL TRY DIFFERENT SUBSTANCES IN DIFFERING PROPORTIONS; IT DOES NOT MEAN YOU HAVE FAILED IF YOUR CONCOCTION IS NOT THAT WHICH YOU EXPECTED! IT SIMPLY MEANS YOU HAVE EXPERIMENTED AND YOU WILL KNOW BETTER NEXT TIME. WHEN YOU EXPERIMENT, WHETHER MAGIC OR ALCHEMY, YOU MUST KEEP AN ACCURATE RECORD IN YOUR GRIMOIRE. IT IS IMPERATIVE AND I CANNOT STRESS THIS ENOUGH. WITHOUT A GRIMOIRE, THE MAGICIAN IS DOOMED TO REPEAT UNDESIRED OUTCOMES OF THE PAST.

YOU MUST RECORD EACH AND EVERY MAGICAL OPERATION THAT YOU CONDUCT. YOU MUST ANALYZE PRACTICES TO DETERMINE IF THOSE ARE SUCCESSFULLY WORKING AND ACHIEVING YOUR

DESIRED RESULTS. THROUGH THIS ANALYSIS, YOU WILL FIND THE BEST RESULTS POSSIBLE AND BY THINKING THROUGH YOUR PROCESSES WHILE ANALYZING THEM, YOU MAY VERY WELL DISCOVER THE SHORTCOMING THAT IS EASILY CORRECTED; ALLOWING YOUR NEXT ATTEMPT TO BE SUCCESSFUL.

LEARNING MAGIC MAY BE A STRUGGLE FOR SOME AND IT WILL BE EASIER FOR OTHER PEOPLE WHO ARE CHALLENGED BY OTHER THINGS THAT MAY TAKE TIME AND PATIENCE IN ORDER TO MASTER. IF YOU ARE NOT GIFTED IN MATH OR SCIENCE, YOU MAY BE STRONGER PERFORMING THE RITUAL; IF YOU ARE NOT STRONG IN THE DELIVERY OF THE RITUAL, YOU MAY BE STRONGER IN ALCHEMY; IF YOU'RE NOT STRONG IN EITHER OF THESE AREAS, PERHAPS YOU HAVE A BETTER ABILITY TO ARRANGE CERTAIN EVENTS INTO A LOGICAL OR CHRONOLOGICAL ORDER.

WE ARE ALL INDIVIDUALS WITH DIFFERENT STRENGTHS AND WEAKNESSES. EMBRACE YOUR INDIVIDUALITY BECAUSE IT IS WHAT MAKES YOU.........YOU. DO NOT FEAR BEING DIFFERENT; THAT IS THE ATTRIBUTE THAT MAKES EVERYONE ELSE WANT TO FOLLOW YOU!

IGNIS IN VITAE

FOR THE SOLE PRACTITIONER, MAGIC IS OFTEN A CHALLENGE. IF YOU ARE IN A COVEN, YOU MAY DRAW UPON THE STRENGTHS OF OTHER COVEN MEMBERS; SOMETHING YOU CANNOT DO WHEN YOU PRACTICE MAGIC ALONE.

HAVING COVEN MEMBERS ALSO HELPS WHEN ANALYZING THE RESULTS OF A RITUAL. SOMETIMES VERY SMALL THINGS ARE OVERLOOKED BY ONE PERSON BUT IN A COVEN SETTING, SOMEONE MAY NOTICE THAT WHICH ANOTHER DID NOT AND THAT MAY BE THE KEY TO UNLOCKING THE SUCCESS OF A SPECIFIC PROCESS. IF YOU LEARN YOUR STRENGTHS AND KNOW YOUR WEAKNESSES, YOU CAN TRULY DEAL WITH EITHER ONE COMPETENTLY AND YOU WILL TRULY FIND THE MASTERY OF MAGIC IS RELATIVELY EASY.

I HOPE THAT WILL BE THE CASE FOR YOU; THE READER. YOU ARE INVESTING YOUR TIME, MONEY AND ENERGY IN SOMETHING THAT YOU ARE DEMONSTRATING THROUGH FAITH. YOUR DESIRES WILL COME TRUE AND I APPLAUD YOU AS SATAN REWARDS YOUR EFFORTS; REACHING OUT AS YOU

DEMONSTRATE YOUR NEED, DESIRE AND WILLING-
NESS TO DO WHAT IS NEEDED TO FULFILL BOTH.

IF YOU SIMPLY CONTINUE LEARNING AND
PRACTICE WHAT YOU HAVE LEARNED, YOU WILL BE
BLESSED WITH SUCCESS. ALWAYS RECORD IN YOUR
GRIMOIRE THAT WHICH YOU HAVE PRACTICED. LAT-
ER, ANALYZE WHAT YOU HAVE RECORDED AND
LEARN 'WHAT WORKS AND DOES NOT WORK'; IT IS
THAT SIMPLE.

YOU MAY HAVE PURCHASED THIS BOOK TO BET-
TER UNDERSTAND SATAN AND DEMONS. I BELIEVE
THAT YOU WILL FULFILL THAT DESIRE ONCE YOU
HAVE READ THE CONTENTS OF THE BOOK. IF YOU
WISH TO BETTER UNDERSTAND HOW TO BECOME A
SATANIST, I WOULD CERTAINLY REFERRED YOU TO
THE VERY FIRST VOLUME OF THIS SERIES; "SANC-
TUM OF SHADOWS VOLUME I: THE SATANIST".

I WILL MAKE CERTAIN ASSUMPTIONS BASED
UPON HAVING READ VOLUME I AND I WILL FUR-
THER MAKE ASSUMPTIONS THAT YOU HAVE READ
MY BOOK OF SATANIC RITUAL. WITHIN VOLUME
1: THE SATANIST AND THE BOOK OF SATANIC RITU-
AL THE FOUNDATION WILL BE LAID DOWN FOR
YOU TO BETTER UNDERSTAND WHAT WILL BE DIS-

CUSSED IN THIS VOLUME.

"WE MUST BEGIN OUR JOURNEY SOMEWHERE ...."

EVERY JOURNEY BEGINS WITH A STEP FORWARD. IF YOU READ THIS VOLUME ALONE (WITH NO OTHER INPUT) AND YOU HAVE FAILED TO READ VOLUME 1: THE SATANIST, YOU WILL CERTAINLY BE AT A LOSS SINCE THE SUBJECT MATTER IS VERY COMPLEX. YOU MUST BEGIN WITH SOME BASICS AND WORK UP TO THE MORE ADVANCED PROCESSES, TOOLS, AND TECHNIQUES.

YOU HAVE MADE A CONSCIOUS DECISION TO LEARN ABOUT SATAN AND DEMONS BY PURCHASING THIS BOOK. I WILL PROVIDE THE INFORMATION HOWEVER, YOU MUST LEARN THE CORRECT METHODS TO APPLY THIS INFORMATION PROPERLY IN ORDER TO ACHIEVE YOUR DESIRED RESULTS.

MAGICAE FIRMITAS

ONE BOOK ALONE WILL NOT TEACH YOU EVERYTHING YOU WILL NEED TO KNOW ABOUT COMMUNICATING WITH SATAN AND DEMONS. FOR THAT REASON, I WILL SAY, THOSE WHO ARE WANTING AND WILLING TO KNOW ABOUT SATANISM, PERFORM YOUR DUE DILIGENCE AND APPROACH THE SUBJECT METHODICALLY. DO NOT FOOL YOURSELF INTO THINKING THIS BOOK WILL TEACH EVERYTHING YOU NEED TO KNOW ABOUT THE SUBJECT......FOR IT WILL NOT. NOR WILL ANY ONE THEOLOGICAL APPROACH FULLY FIT YOUR DESIRES UNTIL YOU REALIZE YOUR TRUE NEEDS.

POSITIVE ENERGY ALWAYS SEEKS POSITIVE ENERGY. LIKE-SOURCES OF ENERGY ARE SIMILAR TO PEOPLE WHO FIND SIMILARITIES BETWEEN EACH OTHER AND THEREFORE, INSTINCTIVELY MIGRATE TOWARD ONE ANOTHER.

IN THE ABSTRACT, ENERGY WILL ALSO FLOW FROM NEGATIVE TO POSITIVE OR FROM POSITIVE TO NEGATIVE. ENERGY IS SOMETIMES UNDERSTOOD AS BEING ALMOST FLUID.

ENERGY WILL SEEK THE PATH OF LEAST RESIS-

TANCE AND MANY TIMES WILL FLOW DIRECTLY INTO A VOID THAT HAS BEEN CREATED BY THE MAGICIAN. IN THIS FASHION, IT IS KNOWN BY THOSE WHO PRACTICE MAGIC THAT BY HARNESSING ENERGY AND CREATING A VOID IN SPACE AND TIME, YOU CAN EASILY MANIPULATE THE ENERGY AND CAUSE IT TO FLOW AS YOU DESIRE.

AS WITH MOVING WATER, ENERGY ALSO WILL GATHER SPEED AND INCREASE IN VOLUME IF IT IS "FUNNELED" INTO A SMALLER SPACE. THE FACT THAT MAGIC IS VERY SIMILAR TO HYDRODYNAMICS, MAKES IT EASY FOR SOME NEW PRACTITIONERS TO VISUALIZE THIS FLOW.

ENERGY CAN BE HARNESSED HOWEVER, IT IS IMPORTANT TO POINT OUT THAT THE FLOW OF ENERGY MUST BE EVALUATED TO ASCERTAIN THE POWER, VOLUME AND ADEQUACY OF THE ENERGY FLOW. IT IS THEREFORE VERY IMPORTANT FOR THE MAGICIAN TO KNOW THE CHARACTERISTICS OF ENERGY DURING AMBIENT CONDITIONS, INDUCED EFFECTS (FORCE) AND WHEN REALIZING MOVEMENT; SUBTLY INCREASING OR DECREASING SPEED, VOLUME AND / OR POWER.

THIS MAY SOUND CONFUSING TO YOU HOW-

EVER, THIS WILL BECOME ABUNDANTLY CLEAR AS YOU DELVE INTO THE STUDY OF ENERGY AND ITS COMPOSITION. THE COMPETENT PRACTITIONER CAN (AND DOES) THIS TO MANIPULATE THE FLOW OF ENERGY. THE PRACTITIONER MUST, I WILL REPEAT, MUST BECOME ACCUSTOMED TO THE CHARACTERISTICS OF ENERGY.

YOU MAY NOT BE ABLE TO SEE ELECTRICITY HOWEVER, IF YOU STICK A METAL OBJECT INTO A WALL OUTLET, YOU WILL REALIZE (QUICKLY) THAT ELECTRICITY HAS AWESOME POWER, EVEN IF "INVISIBLE".

ENERGY BY ITSELF; UNHARNESSED, RAW AND UNTAPPED, AWAITS THE PRACTITIONER BECAUSE THE FORCE OF ENERGY CAN BE TRANSPORTED THROUGH THE PARALLAX DIMENSION. IT IS THE METHOD SATANISTS USE TO CONTACT DEMONS AS THEY PERFORM OUR WORKS AND DEALINGS. KNOWING THE PATH OF ENERGY CAN GREATLY ENHANCE YOUR COMMUNICATION WITH THOSE WHO ARE WILLING (QUID PRO QUO) TO LEND THEIR SERVICES.

FOR THOSE WHO ARE CONFUSED BY THE WORDS I AM WRITING, I WOULD SUBMIT THIS; YOU MUST BECOME KNOWLEDGEABLE AND PROFICIENT IN EN-

ERGY TO WORK SUCCESSFUL MAGICAL PROCESSES. ENERGY MANIPULATION IS CONSIDERED TO BE A BASIC (IF NOT THE MOST BASIC) MAGICAL OPERATION.

YOU WILL PROBABLY REMEMBER I HAVE MENTIONED SEVERAL TIMES IN MY BOOKS A MAGICIAN MUST GROW IN KNOWLEDGE AND ABILITY IN ORDER TO ACHIEVE COMPETENCY IN THE HIGHER SATANIC MAGIC PROCESSES. THESE PROCESSES ARE BUILT UPON BASIC MAGIC PROCESSES (OPERATIONS). WITHOUT A FOUNDATION, THE MAGICIAN CANNOT HOPE TO IMPROVE NOR ACHIEVE WHAT IS SET OUT TO ACCOMPLISH DURING RITUALS.

HERE IS A SECRET; DEMONS ARE DRAWN TO ENERGY. YOU MAY HAVE READ ABOUT PEOPLE WHO HAVE EXPERIENCED A "UNNATURAL BEING" OR WHAT THEY CALL A "GHOST". THIS MAY BE BECAUSE HE / SHE HAS DABBLED IN MAGIC; PERHAPS A TEENAGER TRYING TO WORK A SPELL OR PERHAPS IT WAS A NEW WITCH WHO HAD VENTURED OUTSIDE OF HIS / HER COMPETENCIES; BEGINNING TO EXPERIMENT IN THE BLACK ARTS.

NONETHELESS, THE PRACTITIONER SHOULD KNOW CERTAIN THINGS MUST BE DONE IN ORDER

TO PROTECT HIM OR HERSELF DURING ENERGY MANIPULATION AND MAGICAL WORKINGS. IT IS NOT WITHIN THE SCOPE OF THIS BOOK TO TEACH BASIC MAGICAL OPERATIONS SUCH AS PROTECTION; PERHAPS THAT WILL BE A FUTURE BOOK.

FOR THOSE WILLING TO ACCEPT THAT CHALLENGE AND BEGIN THE JOURNEY OF THE SATANIC, I SAY "BRAVO"! I ENCOURAGE YOU TO PRACTICE THESE THINGS YOU WILL LEARN BUT DO NOT TRY TO DO TOO MUCH, TOO QUICKLY. MAGIC IS POWERFUL; MAGIC IS POTENT; FOR THOSE OF US WHO 'WILL' AND MANIPULATE MAGIC, WE ARE THE MOST POWERFUL ON THE FACE OF THIS EARTH!

FROM A SATANIC ASPECT, USE OF MAGICAL ENERGY IS TRANSFERRED WITH DEMONS. YOU SIMPLY CAN NOT SEND RAW ENERGY ACROSS THE WORLD AND BRING YOUR DESIRES TO FRUITION. WITHOUT A FAMILIAR[7], YOU WILL NOT BE ABLE TO TRANSFER OR RECEIVE THOSE BENEFITS FROM YOUR WORKINGS. A FAMILIAR MAY BE A DEMON, ANIMAL OR ANOTHER PERSON WHO IS UNDER YOUR MAGICAL INFLUENCE.

THE FAMILIAR IS MOST IMPORTANT, FOR WITH-

---

[7] *http://satanicmagic.wordpress.com/2012/08/24/gates-of-hell/* - Satanic Magic Blog

OUT FAMILIARS, YOU WILL NOT SUCCEED IN THE PRACTICE OF MAGIC. IF YOU ARE SIMPLY SEARCHING FOR RICHES AND POWER, SATANISM CAN CERTAINLY PROVIDE THOSE DESIRES HOWEVER, YOU MUST WORK AND EARN THOSE THINGS MAGICALLY! IT IS NOT AN EASY FIX, AS SO MANY PEOPLE BELIEVE. YOU CANNOT MUMBLE A FEW WORDS AND CAUSE THE ENTIRE UNIVERSE TO BEND TO YOUR 'WILL'.

WHAT A MAGICIAN DOES TRULY REQUIRES KNOWLEDGE, DEDICATION, PRACTICE, STUDY AND INVESTMENT ON A DAILY BASIS. MANY OF US HAVE INVESTED A LIFETIME TO REACH MAGICAL PROFICIENCY AND EFFECTIVENESS. DO DELUSIONAL FOOLS REALLY BELIEVE THIRTY MINUTES SURFING THE INTERNET WILL PRODUCE THEIR DESIRES?

IN PART II OF THIS BOOK, I HAVE PROVIDED THE NAMES AND CHARACTERISTICS OF MY FAVORITE DEMONIC BEINGS. THE REFERENCES MAY SEEM TO BE QUITE CONFUSING HOWEVER, AS YOU LEARN AND EXPAND YOUR COGNITIVE POWERS, WHAT SEEMED TO BE WRAPPED IN MYSTERY AND RIDDLES WILL SLOWLY BECOME CRYSTAL CLEAR.

BEAR IN MIND, THE DESCRIPTIONS OF THESE

DEMONS (AND INTERACTIONS) ARE MY PERSPEC-
TIVES; HOW I HAVE EXPERIENCED AND INTERACTED
WITH THE PARTICULAR DEMON. I AM NOT WRIT-
ING A "POPULAR BELIEF" OR DEMONIC ARTIFACT
ARTICLE. YOU MAY DISAGREE WITH MY ASSESS-
MENTS HOWEVER, DO NOT SOPHOMORICALLY
CLAIM I AM WRONG BECAUSE MY EXPERIENCE
DOES NOT ALIGN WITH YOUR PERSONAL BELIEFS OR
IN ANOTHER AUTHOR'S WRITINGS.

YOUR JOURNEY IS EXCITING, FILLED WITH
GREAT EXPERIENCES AND AS YOU BEGIN, I SINCERE-
LY WISH YOU THE BEST OF LUCK. REMEMBER, I
AM WITH YOU, JUST AS SATAN AND THE DEMONS,
AND WITH TIME, YOU WILL BE SUCCESSFUL; I
HAVE NO DOUBT!

NOW, FOCUS YOUR ENERGY, PREPARE YOUR
MIND AND MOVE FORWARD ON YOUR WONDER-
FUL SATANIC JOURNEY.

IN NOMINE DIABOLI

"ONE ATTRIBUTE I HAVE NOTICED ALMOST EVERY TIME DURING DEMONIC MANIFESTATION IS A TEMPERATURE CHANGE. WHEN WEARING A ROBE (AS WORN DURING ALL RITUALS AND RITES) ONE TENDS TO NOTICE THE SLIGHTEST VARIATION IN THE ENVIRONMENT. I HAVE WITNESSED SUCH A DRASTIC CHANGE, CAUSING A HOT AND HUMID SUMMER NIGHT TO TURN ALMOST FROSTY; TO THE POINT THAT I COULD SEE MY BREATH IN THE CANDLELIGHT AND FIRELIGHT."[8]

ALEISTER NACHT

MANY YEARS BEFORE HUMANS DISCOVERED HOW ENERGY WORKS, IT WAS ONCE BELIEVED DEMONS WERE OUR ANCESTORS. IT WAS ALSO BELIEVED DEMONS WERE RESTLESS SPIRITS THAT ROAMED THE FACE OF THE EARTH, LOOKING FOR THEIR FINAL RESTING PLACE. AS HUMANS HAVE EVOLVED, WE HAVE DISCOVERED THESE ENERGY

[8] *A Satanic Grimoire* by Aleister Nacht

FORCES ARE SEEKING A PATH OF LEAST RESISTANCE; THE SAME POLARITY. CONTROLLING THE EBB AND FLOW OF ENERGY IS THE ULTIMATE GOAL OF THE SATANIC MAGICIAN. IF YOU CONTROL THIS FLOW, YOU WILL BE ABLE TO DO GREAT THINGS AND MOLD REALITY TO YOUR 'WILL'. YOU MUST UNDERSTAND ENERGY IS AT THE VERY CENTER OF THE REALITIES YOU HAVE BEEN SEARCHING TO FIND.

DEMONS HAVE EXISTED FOR MILLENNIA. DEMONS ARE SATAN'S MOST DEDICATED PERFORMERS; WHEN I SAY PERFORMER, I DO NOT MEAN AS A TRAINED ANIMAL, I MEAN THIS IN THE STRICTEST FORM OF THOSE WHO PRODUCE RESULTS.

THERE IS NO REASON FOR A SATANIST'S MAGICAL ACTIONS TO BE UNPRODUCTIVE. LAZINESS IS NOT SATANIC; BLAMING SOMEONE ELSE FOR YOUR LACK OF RESULTS IS NOT SATANIC! YOU MUST ACCEPT ACCOUNTABILITY, TAKE ACTION AND LEARN SO YOU MAY ACHIEVE THAT WHICH YOU DESIRE.

WITHOUT SATAN'S POWER, THERE IS NO SATANIC MAGIC! YOU WILL BE INEPT PERFORMING EFFECTIVE SATANIC RITUALS AND YOU WILL NEVER KNOW THE TRUE ESSENCE OF MAGIC UNTIL YOU BELIEVE. ATHEISTS DO NOT HAVE SATANIC POW-

ERS..........PERIOD!! THEY ARE ALSO MOST VUL-
NERABLE TO THE TRUE MAGICIAN'S POWERFUL IN-
FLUENCES AND ARE OFTEN MANIPULATED EASILY
FROM A DISTANCE.

SOME HAVE VIEWED DEMONS AS GREMLINS
AND OTHERS BELIEVE DEMONS FAVOR IMAGES IN
OLD PICTURES OF CARICATURES FROM OLD LITERA-
TURE. REST ASSURED, A DEMON INVOKED WILL
MANIFEST IN WHAT EVER FORM HE / SHE DESIRES.

IN MY EXPERIENCE, DEMONS MANIFEST
THEMSELVES IN HUMANISTIC FORM THAT DOES
NOT LACK ANY DEPTH OR DIMENSION. A DEMON'S
APPEARANCE IS INITIALLY FELT BY A CHANGE OF
TEMPERATURE WITHIN THE SATANIC SANCTUM[9]. I
HAVE ALWAYS NOTICED A DECREASE IN TEMPERA-
TURE; TO THE POINT OF BEING ABLE TO SEE ONE'S
BREATH AS A VAPOR IN THE ATMOSPHERE. THE
SLIGHTEST CHANGE IN TEMPERATURE HAS AN EF-
FECT ON THE ENERGY WITHIN THE SANCTUM. I
WOULD LIKE TO USE AN ANALOGY FOR ILLUSTRA-
TIONAL PURPOSES.

FOR THOSE WHO ARE FAMILIAR WITH METEO-
ROLOGY, IT IS INTERESTING TO NOTE A THUNDER-

---

[9] A private place where one is free from intrusion

STORM CHANGES ITS FORM, POWER AND TRAJECTO-RY BASED UPON CHANGES IN AMBIENT TEMPERA-TURE. THIS TEMPERATURE INVERSION WITHIN THE ATMOSPHERE CAUSES LIGHTNING, WIND, RAIN AND HAIL. THE MOLECULES OF WATER VAPOR GO UP AND DOWN THROUGH THE ASCENDING AND DE-SCENDING AIR SHAFTS OF A CUMULONIMBUS CLOUD; INCREASING SIZE AND WEIGHT WITH EACH REVOLUTION.

AS HEAT IS ADDED FROM THE SUN, THE CLOUD GROWS TALLER AND TALLER. AT SOME POINT, THE WATER VAPOR WITHIN THE CLOUD BEGINS TO BE PROJECTED ABOVE THE THE FREEZING LEVEL IN THE ATMOSPHERE. THE WATER DROPLET FREEZES INTO A SMALL ICE DROPLET WHICH BECOMES TOO HEAVY TO BE CARRIED BY THE UPDRAFT ANY LONGER. IT FALLS THROUGH THE CLOUD AS ICE, MELTING ON THE DECENT INTO A RAIN DROP. THOSE LARGER ICE PELLETS FALL THROUGH (OR OUTSIDE) THE CLOUD AS HAIL.

LIGHTNING ALSO USES SUBTLE CHANGES IN ATMOSPHERIC TEMPERATURE. WHEN THE MOLE-CULES OF WATER BEING TRANSPORTED BY UPDRAFTS AND DOWNDRAFTS REACH A CERTAIN SIZE, FRIC-

TION CREATED WITHIN THE CLOUD CAUSES ELECTRI-
CAL STATIC. WHEN THE STATIC IS BUILT UP TO A
CERTAIN POINT, THE STATIC DISCHARGES AS AN ARC,
BEING ATTRACTED TO A GROUND IN THE FORM OF A
LIGHTNING BOLT. A RAPID EXPANSION AND COM-
PRESSION OF THE AIR AROUND THE LIGHTNING BOLT
CAUSES THE DELAYED CLAP OF THUNDER. YOU SEE
THE LIGHTNING BOLT BEFORE HEARING THE THUN-
DER BECAUSE LIGHT TRAVELS FASTER THAN SOUND;
THUS THE DELAY, DEPENDING ON HOW FAR FROM
THE LIGHTNING BOLT YOU TEND TO BE.

THE SATANIST CAN TAKE THE SAME INFORMA-
TION AND UNDERSTAND HOW A DEMONIC SPIRIT
CAN TRANSGRESS AND MOVE BETWEEN ONE REALI-
TY AND ANOTHER REALITY. A DEMON CAN BE VI-
SUALIZED AS THE WATER DROPLET IN THE ILLUSTRA-
TION. THE DEMON MAY MOVE QUICKLY FROM
ONE PLACE TO ANOTHER BY PASSING THROUGH A
DIMENSION CAUSING A CHANGE OF ATMOSPHERIC
TEMPERATURE TO OCCUR. THE ENERGY SEEKS THE
PATH OF LEAST RESISTANCE AND BECAUSE OF THE
SUDDEN EXPANSION AND COMPRESSION OF AIR
MOLECULES, THE DIMENSION AROUND THE DEMON
SIMPLY 'GIVES WAY' AND REFORMS.

THIS IS A VERY SIMPLE ANALOGY. YOU DO NOT HEAR THUNDER WHEN A DEMON TRANSVERSES THE PARALLAX DIMENSION HOWEVER, YOU WILL SEE LIGHT AND A CHANGE OF COLOR WITHIN THE INNER SANCTUM AREA AND YOU WILL CERTAINLY FEEL THE TEMPERATURE CHANGE. THESE ARE TWO INDICATORS THAT A DEMONIC PRESENCE IS ENTERING OUR DIMENSION.

JUST AS THE MIGHTY LIGHTNING BOLT CONNECTS WITH THE EARTH, THE MIGHTY DEMON CRASHES INTO OUR DIMENSION. THIS MAY SOUND EXTREMELY SIMPLISTIC AS AN EXPLANATION HOWEVER, IT IS THE EASIEST WAY TO UNDERSTAND HOW DEMONIC BEINGS TRANSCEND OUR LIMITED, DIMENSIONAL BOUNDARIES.

THESE ENTITIES ARE HIGHLY EVOLVED AND THE MANNER IN WHICH THEY MOVE GRACEFULLY BETWEEN OUR REALITY AND SATAN'S DOMINION MAY BE QUITE DIFFICULT FOR YOU TO GRASP AT FIRST. WE CANNOT TRANSVERSE THE DIMENSIONAL BOUNDARIES IN PHYSICAL FORM HOWEVER, SATANISTS USE ASTRAL PROJECTION TO TRAVEL TO OTHER DIMENSIONS, BEING ACCOMPANIED BY SATAN OR ONE OF HIS TRUSTED DELEGATES.

THE BATTLE OF GOOD AND EVIL HAS BEEN IN PROGRESS FOR AEONS AND WILL CONTINUE LONG AFTER YOU AND I HAVE JOINED THE OFFICIAL RANKS ACCORDING TO OUR INDIVIDUAL ATTRIBUTES, SKILLS AND ABILITIES.

FOR THE FOLLOWERS OF ESTABLISHED CONTROLLING BELIEF SYSTEMS, YOU MUST UNEQUIVOCALLY BOW DOWN AND WORSHIP THOSE WHO HAVE WRANGLED THE HUMANISTIC POWER THROUGH MANIPULATION AND IN SOME CASES, MURDER ITSELF. MAKE NO MISTAKE, THE ESTABLISHED CHURCH WANTS TO "OWN" YOU; BODY, MIND AND POSSESSIONS.

AS DICTATED IN THEIR BIBLE, TORAH AND OTHER STORY BOOKS, THOSE DESIRING TO SEE THE GATES OF THEIR LITERAL HEAVEN MUST WHOLEHEARTEDLY SUBMIT TO ANY ASININE ORDER OR COMMAND, NO MATTER HOW CRAZY OR UNREALISTIC. THESE GRAND LIES ARE NOTHING MORE THAN MIND CONTROL AND PURE INSANITY; CALLING FOR A FATHER TO MURDER HIS SON, ARMIES TO RAPE WOMEN AND GIRLS IN MASS NUMBERS, STEAL LAND AWAY FROM THEIR PEACEFUL NEIGHBORS WHO WISHED FOR NOTHING MORE THAN PEACE.

WILL RIPPING THE FORESKIN FROM THE PENIS TRU-
LY SATISFY A BLOOD LUST CREATED CENTURIES AGO
BY THE CRIMINALLY INSANE?

HUMANS SHOULD BE SMARTER THAN TO BE-
LIEVE IN SUCH CRYPTIC, BACKWARD IDEAS HOWEV-
ER, RELIGION CONTINUES TO TORTURE AND EN-
SLAVE POPULATIONS OF ALL COUNTRIES ON THE
FACE OF THIS EARTH. I SAY "NO MORE"! IT IS TIME
FOR THE VOICE OF REASON AND SANITY TO SPEAK
OUT AGAINST SUCH NEANDERTHALOID STUPIDITY.

THE TIMES OF BELIEVING SUCH LIES SHOULD BE
A THING OF THE PAST. SHOULD EDUCATED MEN
AND WOMEN BELIEVE A GOD-LIKE CREATURE IS GO-
ING TO ALLOW THEM INTO HIS HEAVEN FOR SIM-
PLY WALKING DOWN AN AISLE OR HAVING WATER
SPLASHED IN THEIR FACES?

THIS IS NOTHING MORE THAN A FABRICATION;
SIMPLISTICALLY SOLD TO SIMPLISTIC MINDS TO JUS-
TIFY ALL THE EVIL THINGS THAT HAPPEN IN THIS
WORLD. WILL SOME CREATURE PROVIDE VIRGINS
AND HONEY DURING AN AFTERLIFE FOR ENDING
HIS / HER OWN LIFE.

SUMMUM MALUM

THERE ARE DEMONS WHO AWAIT YOUR SINCERE CALL. WHETHER YOU HAVE CALLED UPON THEM BEFORE OR YOU ARE PLANNING YOUR FIRST ATTEMPT, YOU SHOULD KNOW THEY ARE WAITING AND WATCHING. YOU CAN TAKE COMFORT IN THEIR PRESENCE; AS THEY ARE FREQUENTLY AT ARM'S LENGTH, SIMPLY ONE DIMENSION REMOVED.

FEAR IS VERY NATURAL WHEN BEGINNING YOUR JOURNEY INTO INVOCATION AND EVOCATION. BEFORE GOING FURTHER, WE SHOULD SET THE FOUNDATION WITH AN EXPLANATION OF WHY THESE WORDS ARE NOT SYNONYMOUS. BOTH OF THESE WORDS CONTAIN THE ROOT OF "VOCARE"; IN LATIN MEANING "TO CALL FORTH".

WHEN AN ENTITY IS SUMMONED BY A PRACTITIONER WHO IS NOT CONNECTED IN SOME MANNER TO THE ENTITY, AN EVOCATION IS THE PROPER TERM TO BE USED. THE ENERGY USED TO PERFORM THE EVOCATION IS "EXTERNAL" TO HIS / HER BODY. THE LEVERAGING OF EXTERNAL ENERGY CREATES AN EASY WAY TO REMEMBER THE DIFFER-

ENCE; "EXTERNAL = EVOCATION".

OBVIOUSLY, THE CONVERSE IS TRUE WHEN DEFINING INVOCATION; INTERNAL POWER IS USED BY THE PRACTITIONER TO CONJURE AN ENTITY THAT IS FAMILIAR AND INTERNALLY RAISED WITH THE INTENTION OF INHABITATION OR POSSESSION OF THE PRACTITIONER'S BODY. THE LEVERAGING OF INTERNAL ENERGY CREATES AN EASY WAY TO REMEMBER THE DIFFERENCE; "INTERNAL = INVOCATION".

THE "DEMON'S HOLE" (OCULUS) IS AN OPENING IN THE CEILING OF THE SATANIC SANCTUM WHICH NOT ONLY ALLOWS SMOKE TO RISE AND ESCAPE BUT ALSO SERVES AS A VISUAL PORTAL WHILE CONJURING SATANIC ENERGY AND CALLING FORTH DEMONS. THE OCULUS WAS VERY APTLY NAMED BY OUR PAGAN ANCESTORS OF THE MAGICAL ARTS.

DEMONS ARE MOST COMMONLY CALLED UPON FOR EITHER EVOCATION OR INVOCATION WHICH CAN CREATE THE FEAR MENTIONED EARLIER. THE VAST MAJORITY OF "FIRST TIME EXPERIENCES" ARE EVOCATIONS, SIMPLY BECAUSE A CERTAIN PROFICIENCY LEVEL MUST BE ACHIEVED BY THE PRACTITIONER BEFORE SUCCESSFUL INVOCATION CAN BE

REALIZED. MUCH GREATER CONTROL AND SKILL IS NEEDED DURING THE BEGINNING OF THE ACTUAL INVOCATION EVENT; MIND AND MAGICAL CONTROLS ARE A NECESSITY, NOT SIMPLY EXTENDING AN INVITATION TO 'APPEAR'. THE PRACTITIONER OPENS HIS / HER BODY TO ACCEPT THE DEMON, WHO WILL RESIDE "IN THE FLESH". MANY RITUALS INVOLVE INVOCATION AND A LIKE NUMBER INVOLVE EVOCATION.

MANY PRACTITIONERS AROUND THE WORLD HAVE RECORDED PROCESSES FOR BOTH OF THESE MAGICAL PREREQUISITES SINCE BOTH HAVE VAST APPLICATIONS AS A PRELUDE TO MAGICAL WORKINGS. BY ACHIEVING COMPETENCY IN EVOCATION AND INVOCATION, MORE COMPLEX PROCESSES 'COME ALIVE' ON THE PAGES OF YOUR GRIMOIRE.

"THERE IS AN INTERESTING PHENOMENA WHICH OCCURS IN MAGIC AND WHICH INVOLVES THE CREATION OF THOUGHT-FORMS. THE MAGICIAN CAN CREATE AN IMAGE WITHIN HIS SUBJECTIVE MIND AND "IMPOSE" IT UPON THE OBJECTIVE WORLD SO THAT IT INFLUENCES THE SUBJECTIVE MINDS OF ALL THOSE INDIVIDUALS WHO COME INTO CONTACT WITH IT. OBJECTS MAY BE CHARGED WITH THIS MAGICAL ENERGY AND BECOME "CHARMED" OR "CURSED". WITHIN A MAGICAL GROUP OR COVEN A GROUP-CONSCIOUSNESS DEVELOPS AND ACTS AS IF IT WERE AN INDIVIDUAL ENTITY."[10]

---

[10] *The Demonic Bible* by Magus Tsirk Susej

AB INITIO VERITAS

A REVELATION OFTEN CALLS A PERSON TO REEVALUATE BELIEF STRUCTURES. IT IS IMPORTANT A PERSON TRULY UNDERSTAND HIS / HER BELIEFS AND BE WILLING TO OVERLOOK CERTAIN ESTABLISHED NORMS IN ORDER TO FIND THE 'TRUTH'. YOUR PARENTS MAY HAVE LOVED YOU HOWEVER, THEY MAY HAVE HARMED YOU MORE THAN YOU WILL EVER KNOW. FOR THIS REASON, THEY MAY HAVE EXPOSED YOU TO CERTAIN LIES AND DOGMA THAT SIMPLY ARE UNTRUE.

I AM NOT IMPLYING YOUR PARENTS WERE EVIL NECESSARILY; I AM SIMPLY POINTING OUT A FLAW; YOUR PARENTS MAY HAVE "BOUGHT INTO" A LIE THEMSELVES. PARENTS USUALLY WANT WHAT IS BEST FOR THEIR CHILDREN HOWEVER, IN SOME THINGS, IT MAY NOT BE BEST FOR A CHILD TO BELIEVE.

I KNOW MANY TIMES IN MY PAST, I WAS FACED WITH THE CHALLENGE OF OVERCOMING YEARS OF SYSTEMATIC RELIGIOUS ABUSE[11] IN ORDER

---

[11] Failure to recognize, provide or attempt to provide adequate or appropriate services, including services that are appropriate to that person's age, gender, culture, needs or preferences.

TO LOOK WELL BEYOND THE SCARS OF MY CHILD-
HOOD RELIGIOUS PRISON CELL.

YOU MUST BE WILLING AND ABLE TO OVER-
COME THE LIES. YOU MUST BE ABLE TO LOOK AT A
NEW THEORY AND EVALUATE IT OBJECTIVELY,
WITHOUT PREJUDICE. IF YOU CANNOT MUSTER
THAT ABILITY, YOU WILL BE LOCKED AWAY IN A
LIFE OF SERVICE TO AN UNLOVING, UNCARING
MASTER. RELIGION IS THAT <u>MASTER</u>!!

SATANISM IS NOT A RELIGION; SATANISM IS A
BELIEF SYSTEM AND I HAVE EXPANDED UPON THIS
SUBJECT IN MY PAST BOOKS AND WRITINGS. IT IS
NECESSARY THE PERSON TRULY UNDERSTAND THAT
WHILE THEIR PARENTS MAY HAVE LOVED THEM
DEEPLY AND DEARLY, THEY ALSO EXPOSED THEM TO
<u>THE MOST EVIL OF ORGANIZATIONS ON THIS EARTH</u>.
MANY LIVES HAVE BEEN TOTALLY DESTROYED BE-
CAUSE OF RELIGION; WHETHER IT IS OLD OR
WHETHER IT IS ESTABLISHED RELIGIONS THROUGHOUT
THE AGES, PEOPLE HAVE SYSTEMATICALLY BEEN EX-
POSED TO EVIL ABUSES, SLAVERY, RAPE AND MUR-
DER.

A WAY TO CONTROL A POPULATION IS THROUGH
POSITIVE CONTROL AND IT IS FOR THAT REASON ES-

TABLISHED RELIGION BRAINWASHES THOSE WHO WILL FOLLOW BLINDLY. BRAINWASHING IS NOT A NEW CONCEPT; IT HAS BEEN USED THROUGHOUT HISTORY. TO QUESTION A RELIGION WOULD BE........TO "BLASPHEME" THAT RELIGION.

ONE OF THE FIRST THINGS A CULT TRIES TO DO IS MAKE ITS MEMBERS UNDERSTAND THAT QUESTIONING ANYTHING IS A SIN. IF YOU CANNOT QUESTION SOMETHING, THEN YOU MUST ACCEPT IT AS BEING TRUTH; THUS CONTROLLING THE PERSON'S PERCEPTION AND BELIEF SYSTEM. HOW MANY PEOPLE EAGERLY AWAIT ARMAGEDDON? HOW MANY PEOPLE WOULD INVITE TOTAL ANNIHILATION OF THE EARTH TO FULFILL THE PROPHECY OF A LUNATIC?

IF YOU CANNOT QUESTION, YOU CANNOT LIBERATE YOURSELF FROM A LIE. IN TODAY'S MODERN SOCIETY, WE EITHER ACCEPT THINGS OR WE REJECT THINGS; YOU MAY BELIEVE CERTAIN THINGS HOWEVER, YOU MUST DECIDE WHAT IS RIGHT FOR YOU. THIS IS IMPORTANT BECAUSE IF YOU DO NOT UNDERSTAND THIS CONCEPT, YOU ARE GOING TO FIND YOU ARE BELIEVING ANYTHING THAT ANYONE SAYS.

KNOWING YOURSELF IS IMPORTANT........IT IS THE MOST IMPORTANT ELEMENT IN SATANIC MAGIC. RELIGIONS HAVE LITERALLY MURDERED PEOPLE OVER TIME. THROUGHOUT HISTORY, RELIGIONS HAVE MADE MARTYRS AND VICTIMS OF THEIR OWN PEOPLE IN ORDER TO FURTHER THEIR AGENDAS. IN FURTHERING THEIR AGENDA, THEY HAVE EAGERLY OFFERED UP THEIR OWN FOLLOWERS TO BE ABLE TO IDENTIFY THEIR PERCEIVED ADVERSARY.

THIS IS A LIE THAT HAS BEEN BELIEVED FOR YEARS AND YEARS; FROM THE MOMENT OF CONCEPTION, A CHILD IS GROOMED TO ACCEPT CERTAIN BELIEFS AS TRUTHS; WHETHER IT IS A MOTHER SPEAKING TO THE UNBORN, TELLING HIM OR HER THEIR MOTHER AND FATHER LOVE THEM. REALIZE ONE THING; YOUR FAMILY MAY VERY WELL OSTRACIZE YOU FOR YOUR UNCONVENTIONAL BELIEFS AND UNWAVERING QUESTIONING OF ALL RELIGIONS.

IF THEY LOVE YOU, THEY WOULD NOT EXPOSE THE YOU TO SUCH ABUSE AT THE HANDS OF ESTABLISHED RELIGION. PARENTS MAY SIMPLY BECOME DELUSIONAL; VICTIMS OF GENERATIONAL PROGRAMMING. MANY OF THESE BELIEFS HAVE BEEN

HANDED DOWN FROM GENERATION TO GENERA-
TION; MANY OF THESE RELIGIONS HAVE NEVER
TRULY BEEN QUESTIONED OR REBUFFED.

WHAT PARENT WOULD GIVE A CHILD TO SEXUAL
PREDATORS? IT CONTINUES TODAY......EVEN
THOUGH WE HAVE UNPRECEDENTED ACCESS TO
KNOWLEDGE AT OUR FINGERTIPS.

SANCTUM OF SHADOWS CORPUS SATANAS

PAX PACIS DE TURBATIO

"ORDNUNG IST DER STAMM EINER GUT GEFÜHRTEN GRUPPE. CAOS ZÜCHTET CAOS UND ZERRÜTTUNG DES ZIRKELS."[12]

"ORDER IS THE ROOT OF A WELL MANAGED GROUP. DISORDER BREEDS DISORDER AND FRAGMENTATION OF THE COVEN."

SILENTIUM IN PERSONA DIABOLI

I HAVE NOT WITNESSED REAL, FACTUAL EVIDENCE OF "CHAOS MAGIC". PERHAPS I HAVE NOT WITNESSED THE RIGHT COVEN HOWEVER, I HAVE NEVER SEEN A SUCCESSFUL MAGICAL WORKING RESULT FROM CHAOS....IN ANY FORM. I HAVE NEVER SEEN ANYTHING PRODUCED FROM CHAOS THAT WAS NOT CHAOS.

THE APPEARANCE OF DEMONS RESULTS FROM A QUIET AND MEASURED APPROACH. THE FIRST TIME

---

[12] The original text of *"Silentium In Persona Diaboli"* spells **chaos** as *"caos"*

A PERSON COMES INTO CONTACT WITH A DEMON (OR SATAN HIMSELF) IS USUALLY DURING OR AFTER HE / SHE HAS SPENT TIME MEDITATING AND IS TRULY CONNECTED WITH THE OTHER SIDE.

THE QUIET AND STILLNESS OF A DEMON OFTEN PRODUCES THE BEST RESULTS. IT IS IMPORTANT TO NOTE, WITHOUT A TRUE UNDERSTANDING OF THE ABILITY TO COMMUNICATE WITH DEMONS, YOU WILL NOT BE ABLE TO EFFECTIVELY SUMMON SATAN NOR DEMONS.

DEMONS ARE INDIVIDUALS, MUCH THE SAME AS YOU AND I HOWEVER, THEY HAVE EVOLVED OVER YEARS AND YEARS OF BEING AND THEY ARE VERY INTELLIGENT; NOT TO BE TAKEN LIGHTLY. ONE OF THE BIGGEST MISTAKES THE SATANIST CAN MAKE IS TO TREAT A DEMON AS AN EQUAL!! THEY ARE FAR TOO EVOLVED AND FAR MORE INTELLIGENT THAN HUMANS. TO DO SO, WILL RESULT IN AN EPIC CATASTROPHE.

MANY PEOPLE HAVE TRIED TO MASTER AND CONTROL THAT DIMENSION ONE STEP FAR REMOVED AND HAVE BEEN COMMITTED TO MENTAL HOSPITALS OR AN EARLY GRAVE........IT IS THAT SIMPLE. YOU MUST USE CAUTION AND BE ABLE TO

REMAIN WITHIN YOUR LIMITATIONS. TO DO SO, YOU MUST FIRST KNOW WHAT THOSE LIMITATIONS ARE.

IT IS QUITE FRIGHTENING TO KNOW THERE ARE PEOPLE WHO CALL UPON DEMONS YET, DO NOT BELIEVE IN THE EXISTENCE OF DEMONS!! THESE INDIVIDUALS ARE SIMPLY PLAYING RUSSIAN ROULETTE!! THE DAY WILL COME WHEN THE DEMON WILL PROVE HIS / HER EXISTENCE......ALTHOUGH IT WILL BE TOO LATE FOR THE HUMAN. NATURAL SELECTION.........SO SHALL IT BE.

SOME DEMONS ARE BENEVOLENT, HAVE A CORDIAL APPEARANCE AND ARE PLEASANT TO BE AROUND. THE INVERSE IS ALSO TRUE. SOME DEMONS WILL MANIFEST THEMSELVES TO A PERSON WHO HAS TAUNTED THEM. IN THIS CASE, THE DEMON ENTERS THE HOST. DEATH OF THE HOST IS CERTAIN.

IN MANY CASES, DEMONS ARE NEITHER EVIL NOR GOOD; THAT DEFINITION IS LEFT TOTALLY TO THE SATANIC PRACTITIONER. I WILL SAY SOME DEMONS WILL SERVE THE PURPOSE OF THEIR SUMMONER BETTER THAN OTHERS; GIVEN, SOME ARE PREDISPOSED TO EVIL AND ARE BETTER ADAPTED TO

SERVE THE WILL OF THE PRACTITIONER SEEKING RE-
VENGE. THIS IS NOT TO SAY THE DEMON IS EASIER
TO WORK WITH.......IT IS NOT!!

DEMONIC PERSONALITIES ARE AS VARIED AS
HUMAN PERSONALITIES. A DEMON MAY OR MAY
NOT SHOW MERCY, EXCITEMENT OR SHARE THE
SAME ENTHUSIASM OR MOTIVES AS THE PRACTI-
TIONER. IT IS UP TO THE SATANIST TO BECOME PRO-
FICIENT IN PRACTICES TO BETTER FOCUS THE ENER-
GY AND SHAPE THE WILL OF THE PRACTITIONER.
FOR THE DEMON CAN PERFORM THE WORK FOR THE
PRACTITIONER HOWEVER, THE PRACTITIONER MUST
KNOW HOW TO DIRECT THE ENERGY.

"GLAUBE ANS UNGLAUBLICHE. DIES IST EINE VORAUSSETZUNG UM MAGISCHE KRAFT ZU STEUERN."

"BELIEVE IN THE UNBELIEVABLE. THIS IS A PRE-REQUISITE OF ENERGY CONTROL."

SILENTIUM IN PERSONA DIABOLI

MANY WHO DABBLE IN THE OCCULT OFTEN ARE DRAWN TO THE IDEA OF CONJURING DEMONIC SPIRITS HOWEVER, THEY MAY NOT KNOW VERY MUCH ABOUT THE OCCULT; PERHAPS THEY MAY HAVE READ THAT A MAGICAL PRACTITIONER HAS THE ABILITY TO CALL UPON DEMONS. THIS MAY SOUND ENTICING AND QUITE ATTRACTIVE; HAV-ING A SPIRT DO HIS OR HER BIDDING! NOT KNOW-ING HOW TO HANDLE A DEMON AFTER IT ARRIVES CAN BE A DETRIMENTAL MISTAKE.....MANY HAVE LIVED TO REGRET.

WHEN I RECEIVE AN EMAIL FROM SOMEONE WHO WANTS TO KNOW HOW TO THROW A SPELL,

CALL UPON THE DARKNESS, WORK ROOTS OR SUMMON A DEMON, I FEEL A CHILL RUN UP MY SPINE. FOR ME TO PROVIDE THIS INFORMATION TO THEM WOULD BE LIKE GIVING THEM A BAZOOKA WITHOUT ANY FURTHER EXPLANATION OF ITS OPERATION.

WHEN A DEMON FIRST MANIFESTS ITSELF, THE PRACTITIONER MAY FALL INTO DISBELIEF AND THIS IS PERFECTLY NORMAL. EVEN FOR THE PRACTITIONER WHO HAS PREPARED ADEQUATELY, THIS SURPRISE AND THE REALITY OF THE SITUATION SOMETIMES CAN OVERWHELM THE SENSES. REMEMBER, DEMONS ARE MYTHOLOGICAL CREATURES TO MOST PEOPLE; MANY PEOPLE DO NOT VIEW DEMONS AS TRUE ANTHROPOMORPHIC BEINGS AND AS SUCH, WHEN MANIFESTED, ARE QUITE FRIGHTENING.

THE ABILITY TO "COME TO TERMS" WITH THE FIRST APPEARANCE OF A DEMON IS A REAL CHALLENGE; AS I'VE SAID BEFORE "MENTAL HOSPITALS AND GRAVEYARDS ARE FULL OF THOSE WHO THOUGHT THEY COULD CONTROL A DEMON AND FOUND OUT TOO LATE THEY COULD NOT". IF YOU'RE GOING TO PLAY, YOU'RE GOING TO HAVE TO PREPARE FOR THE GAME; THAT INCLUDES THE

METAPHORICAL PRICE OF ADMISSION AND IF YOU DO NOT PREPARE, YOU WILL CERTAINLY LOSE!

FOR SOME PRACTITIONERS, LEARNING TO AC- KNOWLEDGE A DEMON IS AS HARD TO DO AS NOT FLINCHING THE EYES WHEN SOMEONE STRIKES YOUR FACE. IT TAKES YEARS OF TRAINING TO TO- TALLY UNDERSTAND CERTAIN ACTIONS THAT CAN BE TAKEN TO CONTROL A DEMON. I HAVE SEEN THOSE WHO THOUGHT DEMONS WERE PETS - THIS IS NOT THE CASE. THESE CREATURES ARE HIGHLY EVOLVED AND ARE NOT ARCHAIC IN THE LEAST BIT.

NEVER FORGET THE DEMON YOU CALL UPON KNOWS YOU; KNOWS ALL OF YOUR SECRETS AND KNOWS YOUR STRENGTHS AND WEAKNESSES. IF YOU BELIEVE YOU CAN CONTROL THE DEMON OR NEGOTIATE THE OUTCOME, YOU ARE ONLY FOOL- ING YOURSELF!

WHILE CREATING AN ENVIRONMENT WHERE A DEMON MAY MANIFEST, DO NOT THINK YOU CAN NEGOTIATE WITH THE BEING. THERE IS ONLY ONE THING THAT THE DEMON WANTS AND THAT IS ONLY WHAT THE DEMON WANTS! YOU MUST ALIGN YOUR WISHES WITH THAT OF THE DEMON'S.

SCIENTIA DONUM DAEMONIS

AN UNDERSTANDING OF SATAN AND DEMONS BEGINS WITH UNDERSTANDING YOURSELF. SATAN AND DEMONS APPROACH EACH AND EVERY HUMAN BEING ON THE FACE OF THIS EARTH IN A DIFFERENT MANNER. THERE IS NO "ONE SIZE FITS ALL" FOR ANYONE. SATAN UNDERSTANDS WE ARE INDIVIDUALS AND WE LEARN THROUGH DIFFERENT METHODS. THERE ARE CERTAIN TECHNIQUES A PERSON MAY USE TO ENABLE THEM TO CLEARLY UNDERSTAND HOW SATAN SPEAKS.

AS THE COMMUNICATION FROM SATAN BECOMES A CLEAR EDUCATION AND LEARNING OF THE SATANIC MANNERISMS AND WAYS THAT SATAN APPROACHES, AN INDIVIDUAL CAN SUBMERGE INTO PERSONAL EXPERIENCE TO CALL HIS / HER VERY OWN.....A METHODOLOGY FOR THE INDIVIDUAL.

HUMANS ARE SUSCEPTIBLE TO GOOD AND BAD INFLUENCES, ESPECIALLY THE UNEDUCATED OR UNTRAINED WHO DOES NOT CLEARLY UNDERSTAND WHERE THEY ARE GOING. THEY MAY BE FOOLED QUITE REGULARLY BY NOT ONLY THE SINISTER BUT

ALSO THE ESTABLISHED CHURCH AS WELL. RELIGIONS OFTEN PREY UPON THE UNWITTING SOUL OF A PERSON THROUGH LIES AND MANIPULATION TECHNIQUES. THESE TECHNIQUES ARE MORE CLEARLY IDENTIFIED BY THE EXPERIENCED HOWEVER, THESE TECHNIQUES ARE NOTHING MORE THAN A SLIGHT OF HAND AND A TRICK THAT IS PLAYED UPON THE UNWITTING AND UNKNOWING.

THIS IS NOT THE ESSENCE OF SATANISM NOR IS IT THE ESSENCE OF HIGHER SATANIC MAGIC; KNOWING WELL SATAN WILL APPROACH AN INDIVIDUAL CANNOT BE CLEARLY DETERMINED FROM SIMPLY READING A BOOK HOWEVER, UNDERSTANDING YOURSELF WILL CERTAINLY HELP YOU TO BRIDGE THAT GAP IN ORDER FOR SATAN TO COMMUNICATE CLEARLY WITH YOU.

SATAN HAS REALLY RECEIVED A BAD RAP AND MOST OF THIS COMES FROM THE ESTABLISHED CHURCH AND THEIR ATTEMPTS TO DEFINE WHO THE "BAD GUY IS"......IN THEIR UNEDUCATED OPINIONS. SATAN IS NOT, I REPEAT...IS NOT, A FIGURE WITH A PITCHFORK AND SCALY RED SKIN. SATAN IS, AMONG OTHER THINGS, ONE OF THE MOST BEAUTIFUL BEINGS IN EXISTENCE. HE HAS, AND

CONTINUES TO BE, A MAJOR INFLUENCE ON THOSE INTELLIGENT AND ARTICULATE INDIVIDUALS WHO MAKE A DIFFERENCE IN OUR WORLD. TRUE DEVIL WORSHIPPERS ARE IN EVERY NATION AND EVERY ORGANIZATION ON THE FACE OF THE EARTH.

SATAN HAS BEEN COLORED THAT OF A LOSER AND IT IS SIMPLY NOT THE CASE! SATAN REVEALS THE TRUTH BUT SINCE MODERN RELIGION IS DESIGNED TO ATTACK ANYTHING THAT IS NOT IN THEIR FAVOR OR CAN COLLECT MONEY FOR THEM, THEY CONTINUE TO FABRICATE WILD STORIES OF KIDNAPPING AND RITUAL MURDER COMMITTED BY SATAN'S FOLLOWERS. SATAN HAS SIMPLY BEEN REDUCED TO A COMIC BOOK FIGURE MEANWHILE, THE ESTABLISHED CHURCH RAPES AND MURDERS AT WILL....ALL IN THE NAME OF THEIR GOD.

MUCH HAS BEEN WRITTEN ABOUT SATAN AND SOME WRITINGS ARE ACCURATE HOWEVER, THE VAST MAJORITY OF BOOKS AND PERIODICALS WRITTEN ABOUT THE KING OF THIS WORLD ARE HIGHLY INACCURATE; BLASPHEMOUS LIES! SATAN IS HIGHLY INTELLIGENT, VASTLY ARTICULATE AND THE MOST TRUTHFUL OF ANYONE YOU WILL EVER KNOW. WHOLEHEARTEDLY, HE GUIDES THOSE WHO SEEK

AND COME TO HIM. HE ONLY WISHES TO REVEAL THE TRUTH TO THOSE WHO ARE INTELLIGENT ENOUGH TO LISTEN.

HE IS THE BIGGEST ADVOCATE FOR HUMANITY THAT EVER WAS OR EVER WILL BE. HE IS TRULY A FRIEND, MENTOR, GUIDE AND A FATHER WHO, WHILE EXERCISING THE ROLES AND DUTIES OF THAT TITLE, WILL CHASTISE THOSE WHO ARE IN NEED. SATAN IS MORE ABOUT "DOING THE RIGHT THING" AND JUSTICE THAN ANY OTHER PERSON OR BEING.

SATAN DOES NOT CARE ABOUT THOSE WHO DO NOT CARE ABOUT THEMSELVES! HE WILL NOT TELL YOU LIES; HE WILL NOT LEAD YOU ASTRAY BY INFLATING YOUR EGO. IF IT IS NOT THE TRUTH, HE WILL NOT "BUTTER YOUR ASS" AND ONE THING IS FOR CERTAIN, HE WILL ADMINISTER JUSTICE SWIFTLY AND APPROPRIATELY TO MEET ANY SITUATION!

HE IS A LOVING FRIEND HOWEVER, HE WILL SHOW YOU ONLY THAT WHICH YOU ARE CAPABLE OF UNDERSTANDING. THIS IS ANOTHER REASON WHY IT IS SO IMPORTANT FOR THE PRACTITIONER TO LEARN, STUDY AND PRACTICE. SATAN WILL NOT GIVE YOU MORE THAN THAT WHICH YOU CAN HANDLE. HE WILL NOT HEAP KNOWLEDGE ONTO

YOU ONLY TO WATCH YOU BUCKLE UNDER THE UNBEARABLE WEIGHT. HE WILL GO AS QUICKLY AS YOU WANT TO GO WHEN LEARNING OR AS SLOWLY AS IS REQUIRED IN YOUR PARTICULAR CASE.

THIS IS HARD FOR SOME SATANISTS TO UNDERSTAND BECAUSE THEY ARE ANXIOUS AND MOTIVATED; THEY WANT TO LEARN HOWEVER, SATAN WILL ONLY GIVE AS MUCH INFORMATION AS YOU CAN SUITABLY DIGEST AND RETAIN. YOU WILL NOT BE ABLE TO UNDERSTAND SOME CONCEPTS IMMEDIATELY AND SATAN KNOWS THAT THEREFORE, HE WILL BUILD THE ADEQUATE FOUNDATION OF KNOWLEDGE ON WHICH YOU MAY BUILD A STABLE AND RESILIENT PRACTICE OF MAGIC.

IF YOU DO NOT FEEL YOU ARE LEARNING AS MUCH AS YOU WANT, THERE IS A REASON. THE FACT IS, YOU MAY BE READING THIS VERY SENTENCE FOR THE FIFTH OR SIXTH TIME; TRYING TO UNDERSTAND THE MEANING OF THIS PASSAGE. UNTIL YOU HAVE A TOTAL GRASP AND HAVE MASTERED WHAT HE WANTS YOU TO MASTER, YOU WILL NOT PROCEED ANY FURTHER IN YOUR STUDIES AND LEARNING. SATAN SETS THE TEMPO; HE HIMSELF SETS THE TONE OF YOUR LEARNING EVENT

SANCTUM OF SHADOWS CORPUS SATANAS

AND OVERALL ACQUISITION OF KNOWLEDGE. HE TRULY KNOWS YOUR ABILITIES AND WHILE YOU MAY THINK YOU CAN HANDLE MORE THAN HE PROVIDES, AS JACK NICHOLSON SAID, "YOU CAN'T HANDLE THE TRUTH!!"

IT IS IMPORTANT FOR YOU TO COME TO TERMS WITH REALITY, AS IT IS NOT A DEROGATORY STATEMENT WHEN SATAN COMMUNICATES "YOU ARE NOT READY FOR THE NEXT CHAPTER, THE NEXT EVENT OR NEXT EXPERIENCE". HE WILL METICULOUSLY BREAK DOWN THE KNOWLEDGE INTO SMALLER ELEMENTS OF WHICH YOU WILL BE ABLE TO UNDERSTAND. HE WILL NOT SET YOU UP FOR FAILURE!

YOUR FRIENDS OR FAMILY MAY SET YOU UP FOR FAILURE YET, SATAN WILL NOT. IF YOU EXPERIENCE FAILURE, REST ASSURED THERE WAS SOMETHING, SOME EVENT, THAT HAPPENED SO YOU SHOULD HAVE RECOGNIZED IT AS A WARNING SIGNAL. HE WANTS YOU TO BE AWARE OF IMPENDING FAILURES; HE WANTS YOU TO KNOW WHAT IS ABOUT TO HAPPEN HOWEVER, YOU MUST PAY CLOSE ATTENTION TO THE SIGNS. HE WILL NOT CALL ON YOUR CELL PHONE NOR WILL HE EMAIL AND

WARN YOU ABOUT SOMETHING YOU SHOULD BE PAYING ATTENTION TO. THAT IS NOT THE WAY COMMUNICATION WITH SATAN OCCURS. HE IS VERY SUBTLE AND IF YOU MISS A COMMUNICATION, IT IS USUALLY BECAUSE YOU CHOSE TO IGNORE IT SIMPLY WERE NOT PAYING ATTENTION.

PRECONCEIVED NOTIONS ARE OFTEN THE CULPRITS WHEN AN EVENT HAPPENS. SOME PEOPLE WILL SIMPLY HAVE AN IDEA AND WILL NOT LOOK, LISTEN NOR YIELD TO REASON OR ANY OTHER SIGNS OR MESSAGES. IN THIS CASE, THE PERSON IS DOOMED TO FAILURE THROUGH HIS / HER OWN WILL. SATAN WILL NOT PLACE YOU INTO HARM'S WAY IF YOU DO NOT DESIRE TO BE THERE. REMEMBER, I HAVE SAID MANY TIMES THAT SATANISM IS NOT ANARCHY. PEOPLE CAN BE HURT AND EVEN KILLED BY THEIR OWN ACTIONS. THEY MAY ATTEMPT TO ASSIGN BLAME TO SATAN. THAT IS HYPOCRITICAL AND NOT SATANIC!!

SATAN DEMANDS YOU ACCEPT RESPONSIBILITY AND ARE ACCOUNTABLE FOR YOUR ACTIONS. HE WILL NOT ACCEPT ANYTHING LESS! HE KNOWS YOU AS AN INDIVIDUAL AND HE KNOWS YOUR DEFENSE MECHANISMS, YOUR DEMEANOR, YOUR

ACTIONS AND HE ALSO KNOWS YOUR INTENTIONS.......YOU CANNOT LIE TO SATAN SO DO NOT TRY.

THERE ARE THOSE WHO ATTEMPT TO LIE TO SATAN EVERY DAY; YOU CANNOT TELL HIM "IF YOU MAKE ME A MILLIONAIRE, I WILL WORSHIP YOU FOREVER!" SATAN IS NOT A FOOL - HE KNOWS YOU BETTER THAN YOU KNOW YOURSELF. HE EVEN KNOWS WHAT YOU WILL DO IN FUTURE SITUATIONS WHICH HAVE NOT CROSSED YOUR MIND AND HE KNOWS YOU WILL DO CERTAIN THINGS; FOR IT IS YOUR VERY HUMANISTIC NATURE.

SO MANY PEOPLE UNDERESTIMATE SATAN'S ABILITIES AND WISDOM. HE HAS BEEN, IS, AND SHALL BE LONG AFTER WE HAVE CEASED TO EXIST IN THIS EARTHLY REALM. TO UNDERESTIMATE HIS POWER AND PERCEPTION, IS TO DO SO AT YOUR OWN RISK.

DO NOT MISUNDERSTAND; SATAN IS NOT TO BE FEARED EXCEPT BY THOSE WHO HAVE REASON TO FEAR HIM. THERE ARE THOSE WHO WOULD TRY TO STEAL FROM OR HURT ANYONE HOWEVER, THEY WILL NOT DO THIS TO SATAN. FOR THOSE PEOPLE

HAVE A REASON TO FEAR SATAN - THEY HAVE VERY GOOD REASON!

SATAN MUST BE RESPECTED; HE HAS EARNED THE RESPECT HE IS DUE. HIS AWESOME POWER DEMANDS RESPECT HOWEVER, HE DOES NOT DEMAND NOR ASK FOR YOUR WORSHIP. THIS IS A COMMON MISCONCEPTION AMONG SATANIST AND OTHER BELIEF SYSTEMS. SATAN DOES NOT WANT YOUR WORSHIP, HE DOES NOT CRAVE YOUR ATTENTION NOR DOES HE NEED YOUR ACKNOWLEDGMENT.

SATAN WANTS YOU TO THINK FOR YOURSELF AND HE DEMANDS THOSE WHO COME TO HIM SHOULD BE PREPARED. HE WILL REACT HARSHLY IF THEY ARE NOT! SATAN DEMANDS YOUR ADVANCEMENT AS A SATANIST; IT IS A REQUIREMENT FOR YOU TO CONTINUE TO GROW, MATURE AND LEARN.

IN SOME CASES, HUMAN STUPIDITY SHOULD RESULT IN IMMEDIATE DEATH; OF THAT I AM CONVINCED. THIS ALSO APPLIES TO SATANISTS. THOSE WHO ARE IGNORANT AND REMAIN IN IGNORANCE WILL FIND THAT OVER TIME, SATAN WILL BECOME DISPLEASED; FOR THEIR LAZINESS IS UNACCEPTABLE TO SATAN. SATAN DOES NOT ACCEPT EX-

CUSES; THE FACT YOU ARE READING THIS INFOR-
MATION RIGHT NOW IS DEMONSTRATING YOUR
DESIRE TO LEARN. CONTINUE ON THAT JOURNEY.

IF YOU CHOOSE TO CONTINUE TO LEARN, HE
WILL RICHLY BLESS AND INCREASE YOUR KNOWL-
EDGE GREATLY; IF YOU DO NOTHING WITH THE
KNOWLEDGE OR YOU DO NOT PURSUE WISDOM
WITH UNDERSTANDING OF THIS PREMISE, HE WILL
FIND THAT UNACCEPTABLE.

YOU ARE IN A CONSTANT STATE OF FLUX; A
FLUID SITUATION THROUGHOUT YOUR LIFETIME
AND YOU ARE EITHER LEARNING OR DEGRADINGLY
STAGNANT. YOU ARE EITHER IMPROVING OR YOU
ARE DECOMPOSING! THERE IS NO STATUS QUO. YOU
MUST UNDERSTAND HE EXPECTS THOSE WHO MAKE
A COMMITMENT TO LIVE UP TO THAT COMMIT-
MENT AND HE WILL NOT ACCEPT ANYTHING LESS.
SATAN DOES NOT ACCEPT EXCUSES NOR DOES HE
CARE ABOUT THE SITUATION YOU MAY BLAME
YOUR CONDITION UPON. HE EXPECTS YOU TO BE
STRONG AND MOVE FORWARD CONSTANTLY, FOR
THAT IS HIS CHARGE TO EACH AND EVERY SA-
TANIST.

THERE IS A PRICE TO PAY AND YOU MUST BE

WILLING TO PAY THAT PRICE IN ORDER TO AD-
VANCE. THERE IS MORE TO SATANISM; THE SATAN-
IC LIFESTYLE AND WORKING DILIGENTLY TO
ACHIEVE KNOWLEDGE AND APPLYING YOUR NEW-
LY GAINED KNOWLEDGE. THIS WILL BRING YOU
CLOSER WITH SATAN AND HE WILL ACKNOWLEDGE
YOUR WORK. HE WILL REWARD YOU GREATLY FOR
THOSE THINGS.

IT IS FOR THIS REASON THAT THOUGH WE HAVE
TECHNOLOGY ALL AROUND US WE ACTUALLY ARE
NOT BECOMING SMARTER OR MORE INTELLIGENT AS
A RESULT. PEOPLE ARE SIMPLY TOO LAZY TO UN-
DERSTAND THE TRUTH.

HAVING INFORMATION AROUND YOU DOES
NOT NECESSARILY MEAN THAT YOU ARE INTELLI-
GENT. BEING ABLE TO ACCESS THE INFORMATION
DOES NOT MEAN YOU ARE SMART; IF YOU DO NOT
USE THE INFORMATION OR IF YOU DO NOT KNOW
HOW TO USE THE INFORMATION, THAT INFORMA-
TION BECOMES WORTHLESS. YOU MUST APPLY CER-
TAIN PRINCIPLES AND TECHNIQUES IN ORDER TO
RECEIVE A RESULT AND IF YOU DO NOT OR WILL
NOT SEE CERTAIN THINGS AS TRUE, YOU WILL
ABATE THE PROCESS.

No one wants to cause trouble all of the time however, if you do not understand truth, you will not be able to apply truth. It is because of this truth that you must accept certain things through faith however, you must never cease to question! You will know magic when you see it. Since you were exposed to it at a very young and tender age, it will be familiar to you even now.

Now find your quiet place in this world and begin to absorb these words. I have asked Satan to bless this subject matter. You will gain vital insight into the Satanic and Demonic world. I believe Satan will accept the offer on your altar if you truly dedicate yourself to learning more about him and the Satanic processes.

CUM TEMPORE MUTAMUR

THE DIFFERENCE IN ATMOSPHERES BETWEEN THE PHYSICAL WORLD AND THE REALITY WORLD OF THE PARALLAX DIMENSION SOMETIMES ALLOWS FOR THE PRACTITIONER TO PEER INTO THAT OTHER AT-MOSPHERE FROM A PERCEPTION STANDPOINT.

A HUMAN BEING LIMITED IN SUCH A WAY AS ONLY TO REALIZE THREE DIMENSIONS IS AT A BIT OF A DISADVANTAGE HOWEVER, DEMONS CAN AND OFTEN DO TRANSVERSE THAT VEIL AND THE EMPTY NEGATIVE SPACE LEFT BEHIND AS THEY MOVE FROM ONE TO ANOTHER REMAINS UN-BACK FILLED, ALLOWING THE PRACTITIONER A VIEW INTO THAT ATMOSPHERIC CHASM.

SOME PRACTITIONERS DESCRIBE THIS AS SEEING STARS, EVEN BLACK STARS, OR WITNESSING WHAT SOME DESCRIBE AS A TOTALLY BLACK VORTEX SUS-PENDED IN SPACE; EMITTING LIGHT FROM THE BOT-TOM OF A SPHERICAL FUNNEL. THESE OBJECTS ALIGN THE ENCLAVE ORIENTATION FOR THE PRACTI-TIONER. IT MAY SEEM FRIGHTENING AND MAY ABSOLUTELY BE OVERWHELMING EXPERIENCING THIS FOR THE FIRST TIME. THE BLACK STARS, AS

SOME DESCRIBE, ARE NOTHING MORE THAN A PER-
CEIVED ILLUSION TO THE PRACTITIONER BECAUSE HE
OR SHE IS ACTUALLY PEERING INTO THE FOURTH
(AND SOMETIMES BEYOND) DIMENSION.

THE FOURTH DIMENSION APPEARS FRAGMENTED
BECAUSE OF OUR HUMAN LIMITATIONS. MUCH
LIKE THE HUMAN EYE CANNOT VIEW THE SMALL-
EST OF PIXELS OR THE HUMAN EAR CANNOT HEAR
THE HIGHEST OR LOWEST OF SONIC FREQUENCIES,
THE PERCEPTION IS LIMITED BY MERELY BEING
HUMAN. A DEMON'S PERCEPTION IS NOT THE
SAME AS OURS; DEMONS CAN VIEW, AS WELL AS
OCCUPY, OTHER DIMENSIONAL SPHERES OR GLOBU-
LAR SHELLS.

DEMONS CAN ALSO NAVIGATE FROM ONE OR-
BICULAR TO ANOTHER. THIS IS ACCOMPLISHED (IN
PART) BY THEIR HIGHLY EVOLVED SENSORY AND
ENERGY-MANIPULATING MULTIMODAL "MODUS
VIVENDI" PROCESSES. THESE PROCESSES ARE VERY
COMPLEX AND MULTIFACETED. THE FACT THAT A
HUMAN BRAIN CANNOT CONCEIVE WHAT I AM
EXPLAINING AT THIS MOMENT, IS SIMPLY THE DEF-
INITION OF BEING HUMAN. BECAUSE YOU ARE
HUMAN, YOU MAY BE HAVING DIFFICULTY UN-

DERSTANDING OR RELATING TO THIS EXPLANATION OF DIMENSIONS. DEMONS DO NOT HAVE OUR LIMITATIONS AND IT IS THROUGH THE LIMITED CAPACITY AND COMPETENCE THAT WE, AS HUMANS, MUST DRAW UPON THE DEMONIC POWERS IN ORDER TO ACCOMPLISH OUR DESIRES THROUGH SATANIC MAGIC.

OUR HUMANISTIC PROCESSES ACTUALLY INTERTWINE WITH THE DEMONIC HIGHER PROCESSES AND THAT OBLIQUE INTERACTION IS THE PRACTITIONER'S "MISSION TO MASTER". IF YOU TAKE ANYTHING AWAY FROM THIS BOOK, YOU MUST UNDERSTAND THIS PREMISE IN WHICH WE, AS PRACTITIONERS, DILIGENTLY WORK. THIS IS THE REASON FOR OUR STUDY AND PRACTICE!

THERE ARE THOSE OF US WHO HAVE ACHIEVED (AND MAINTAIN) A CERTAIN COMPETENCY LEVEL THAT MAY BE FAR MORE ADVANCED THAN THE BEGINNER HOWEVER, AS ADVANCED PRACTITIONERS OF MAGIC, WE ARE CONSTANTLY LEARNING, EVOLVING AND BECOMING. IT IS THIS INHERENT NATURE WHICH FORCES, PUSHES, SHOVES AND APPEALS TO OUR INSTINCTIVELY-DRIVEN, PRURIENT COMPORTMENT TO CALL UPON US; BEING PREDIS-

POSED AND INHUMANELY-INCLINED TO BETTER UNDERSTAND MAGICAL PROCESSES BY RELENTLESS DECOMPOSING, EXTRAPOLATING AND TENACIOUSLY EXAMINING EACH AND EVERY ELEMENT OF THE WHOLE PROCESS.

SATANIC MAGICIANS ARE INSTINCTIVELY DRAWN TO UNDERSTAND MORE AND MORE ABOUT THESE PROCESSES, FORMULATIONS WHILE CONTINUOUSLY IMPROVING AND DISCOVERING NEW METHODS. WE LEARN JUST AS YOU LEARN; IT IS AN ITERATIVE SEQUENCE. WE ARE MORE IN-TUNE OR CONNECTED WITH THE OPPOSITE SIDE; THE DIMENSIONS BEYOND THE VEIL OF WHICH I SPEAK SO OFTEN.

WITHIN THE CHANGES OF THE REALITY LEVELS, IT IS IMPORTANT "I DARE SAY PARAMOUNT" THE PRACTITIONER BECOMES ONE WITH HIS OR HER PROCESSES. MAGIC MUST BE SUSTAINABLE OVER TIME AND IF THE ATTRIBUTE IS ABSENT, THE PRACTITIONER WILL CERTAINLY LOSE ANY ATTAINED PROFICIENCY AND SEEK "ENTERTAINMENT" ELSEWHERE.

FOR A DEMON, THOSE WHO DABBLE IN THE BLACK ARTS ARE ALMOST COMICAL; THEY ARE SIMPLY SMALL CHILDREN WHO HAVE JUST LEARNED TO

STAND BY THEMSELVES; WOBBLY-LEGGED, UN-STEADY, RAMBLING AND BOUNCING FROM PLACE TO PLACE, THING TO THING, AND SUBJECT TO SUB-JECT. THERE IS A WAY HOWEVER, WITH TIME AND EFFORT, YOU CAN IMPROVE YOUR STANCE 'MAGI-CALLY SPEAKING'.

THE INTERACTION WITH DEMONS BUILDS RELA-TIONSHIPS AND THE FOUNDATION ON WHICH TO BUILD A DEEPER, MEANINGFUL INTERACTIONS. THIS WILL RESULT IN A DEEPER UNDERSTANDING AND A SHARING OF KNOWLEDGE.

YOU CANNOT IMPRESS A DEMON WITH YOUR SIMPLISTIC, HUMANISTIC, LIMITED SCOPE ABILITIES NOR YOUR LIMITED COGNITIVE ABILITIES HOWEV-ER, YOU CAN OFFER RECIPROCITY. AS SOCIAL ANI-MALS, HUMANS BUILD RELATIONS WITH OTHERS OF LIKE MINDS. YOU WILL DO THE SAME WITH SPECIF-IC DEMONS OVER TIME.

ALIGNMENT OF HUMAN OBJECTIVES WITH THOSE OF THE DEMONIC AND SATANIC IS MOST IM-PORTANT. DEMONIC RELATIONSHIPS ARE THE SAME "QUID PRO QUO" ALIGNMENTS ALLOWING YOU TO TAKE FULL ADVANTAGE OF THE RESULTING POWER AND POSITION OFFERED TO YOU. IT IS CERTAINLY

AN ACHIEVABLE OBJECTIVE YOU MUST WORK DILI-
GENTLY TOWARD. THIS STATUS COMES WITH A PRICE
HOWEVER; THE REWARDS ARE IMMEASURABLE AND
CERTAINLY WORTH PURSUING. MAKE THE EFFORT
AND SEIZE YOUR REWARD!

FROM THIS REALITY TO THE NEXT REALITY,
YOU CERTAINLY CAN, WITH TIME, DEVELOP THOSE
SKILLS WHICH WILL BE IMPERATIVELY NEEDED AS
YOU PROGRESS IN YOUR MAGICAL STUDIES, CORRE-
LATIONS AND PRACTICE OF THE SATANIC ARTS.

VADE MECUM

THE RITUAL BELL HAS BEEN USED THROUGHOUT HISTORY TO SOUND IN ORDER TO BRING HUMANS TOGETHER. WHETHER IT IS A DINNER BELL OR THE SATANIC BLACK MASS BELL WHICH BRINGS THE WITCHES INTO THE CIRCLE, THE BELL NOTIFIES THOSE WHO ARE LISTENING THAT AN EVENT IS ABOUT TO TRANSPIRE.

FOR THOSE WHO ARE CALLING TOGETHER THE CIRCLE FOR THE PURPOSES OF DEVIL WORSHIP, THE BELL IS MORE SIGNIFICANT THAN JUST A REMINDER OR A NOTIFICATION INSTRUMENT. THE BELL ACTUALLY CLEARS THE AIR OF EXISTING HARMONIC VIBRATIONS SO THE SPACE CAN BE REPLACED WITH LOW-FREQUENCY OSCILLATIONS CREATED BY THE DEVIL WORSHIPER USING "SINISTER CHANT" (SANCTUS).

BECAUSE THE "DEVIL WORSHIPER" DESIRES TO CALL UPON THOSE JUST BEYOND OUR THIRD DIMENSION, CLEARING AND CLEANSING THE AIR RESETS ALL AUDIBLE SOUNDS TO A BASELINE THAT CAN THEN BE MANIPULATED. THE SIGNIFICANCE OF RINGING THE BELL THREE (3) TIMES IN SE-

QUENCE ESTABLISHES A COMMUNICATION TO THE TRAINED EAR AND THUS PROVOKES AN ANIMAL RESPONSE. MUCH LIKE AN OWL WILL CALL ACROSS THE DARK FOREST AND AWAITS A RESPONSE IN KIND, SO DOES THE BELL FOR THE SATANIC COVEN.

YOU MAY THINK OF THE RINGING OF THE BELL AS AN ANALOG EMAIL MESSAGE OR AN ANALOG TEXT MESSAGE (FOR THOSE TECH-SAVVY PEOPLE) FROM LONG AGO. THIS SIMPLISTIC (YET EFFECTIVE) COMMUNICATION METHOD HAS BEEN UTILIZED FOR YEARS AND GENERATIONS; SOUNDING IN ALL DIRECTIONS. THOSE WHO KNOW AND RECOGNIZE THAT FAMILIAR RHYTHM AND TIMBER, INSTINC-TIVELY RESPOND ACCORDINGLY. IT IS BEAUTIFUL MUSIC TO THE SATANIC COVEN.

FOR THOSE WHO HAVE NEVER EXPERIENCED NOR HAVE SATANIC KNOWLEDGE, THE SEQUENCING OF BELLS COMMUNICATE MORE THAN A MEETING. COVENS OF WITCHES NOT ONLY NOTIFIED MEM-BERS OF GATHERINGS BUT ALSO SENT MESSAGES ABOUT THE RITUAL / MEETING SONICALLY.

SPECIAL SOUND INFLECTIONS AND TRANSCRIP-TIONS USING THE WITCHES' ALPHABET WERE CREAT-ED THAT WOULD NOTIFY MEMBERS OF WHEN TO

MEET OR ANY PERCEIVED DANGERS EXPECTED.

IN TODAY'S MODERN SOCIETY, WE CONTINUE TO USE THE BELL AS FORMAL NOTIFICATION WITHIN THE SANCTUM OR WITHIN THE CIRCLE AS A SYMBOL, MUCH AS A GAVEL IS USED BY A JUDGE TO BRING A COURTROOM INTO ORDER. MANY OF THE METHODS OF THE PAST HAVE BEEN LOST FOREVER AND THUS, NEVER REVIVED OR REPLACED; WHICH IS A REAL TRAGEDY.

FROM THE FIRST UNTIL THE LAST TOLL OF THE BELL, THE INNER SANCTUM TAKES ON AN ENTIRELY DIFFERENT COMPOSURE, AMBIENCE AND TONE. AT THE FIRST TOLL, THE SIGNIFICANCE OF THE FORMAL NOTIFICATION BRINGS THE BROTHER/SISTERHOOD INTO ORDER.

THOSE WHO MAY HAVE APPEARED HAPPY, JOVIAL, AND JOKINGLY IRREVERENT ARE IMMEDIATELY CALLED INTO A MORE "SERIOUS STATE OF PERSONAL CONDUCT". THE COVEN COMES TO ORDER FOR A PURPOSE AND EACH INDIVIDUAL'S ATTENTION AND ENERGY MUST BE FOCUSED ON THE TASK(S) AT HAND.

THE RITES AND RITUALS OF DEVIL WORSHIP CALL FOR THE UTMOST SERIOUSNESS. THE SATANIC

SANCTUM IS NOT A PLACE FOR FOOLISHNESS, CHAOS NOR LACKADAISICAL CONDUCT DURING RITE AND / OR RITUAL PERFORMANCES. WE, AS DEVIL WORSHIPERS, ARE GOING ABOUT OUR FATHERS WORK AND THIS WORK IS "SERIOUS BUSINESS". SATAN EXPECTS IT TO TAKEN SO AND NO DEVIATIONS ARE PERMITTED.

THE FINAL TOLL OF THE BELL (THIRD SEQUENCE) NOTIFIES THE COVEN THE RITUAL IS COMPLETE. MUCH AS THE TERMINOLOGY "SO SHALL IT BE" SIGNIFIES THE END OF A MAGICAL WORKING, THE SOUNDING OF THE BELL IS A SIGNAL THAT THE RITE AND / OR RITUAL HAS CONCLUDED.

AN EASIER WAY TO EXPLAIN THIS (FOR THOSE WHO LACK FORMAL RITUAL EXPERIENCE) IS SIMPLY THIS: "THE BELL BRINGS THE COVEN INTO ORDER, CLEARS THE AIR FOR THE COVEN TO REPLACE WITH THEIR SINISTER CHANT, VIBRATIONS AND FREQUENCIES, WHILE IT BRINGS THE DEVIL WORSHIPER INTO A TRANCE-LIKE STATE OF PREPARATION; REPLACING ALL OF THE SOCIALLY-ACCEPTABLE WITH THAT OF THE DEVIL'S OWN DESIRES!

THERE WILL ALWAYS BE THOSE WHO DO NOT BELIEVE IN THE DEVIL OR DEMONS AND FOR THOSE

PEOPLE, LIFE IS <u>UTTERLY</u> HOPELESS. LEARNING ABOUT A SUBJECT SUCH AS DEMONS OR SATAN CAN BE A TAUNTING TASK HOWEVER, FOR THE SAKE OF LEARNING, ACCEPT IT AS A SATANIC CHALLENGE.

YOU MUST <u>FIRST</u> BELIEVE IN SATAN'S EXISTENCE IN ORDER TO WORSHIP SATAN! SO MANY ATHEISTS CALL THEMSELVES SATANISTS, YET HAVE NO CLUE AS TO THE REAL IDENTITY OR POWER OF OUR KING. CLAIMING TO BE A SATANIST WHILE DENYING THE VERY EXISTENCE OF SATAN IS A BLASPHEMY.

WHILE I RESPECT ANTON LAVEY AS A PIONEER, HE CLEARLY DEMONSTRATED THROUGH HIS "SATANISM" THAT HE <u>DID NOT BELIEVE IN ALMIGHTY SATAN</u> NOR DID HE BELIEVE IN DEMONS AND THE ARCHITECTURE OF DEMONOLOGY. THIS IS WHERE MY RESPECT ENDS.

LAVEY WAS A CARNIVAL WORKER WHO SAW AN OPPORTUNITY TO EXPLOIT SOMETHING THAT HAD NOT BEEN PREVIOUSLY EXPLOITED. FOR THIS VERY REASON, IT IS SAFE TO SAY THOSE WITHIN THE ESTABLISHED "CHURCH OF SATAN" DO NOT BELIEVE IN SATAN'S EXISTENCE.

WITHOUT SATAN, THERE CAN BE NO SATANIC

MAGIC! THE MAGIC LAVEY MENTIONED IN HIS SATANIC BIBLE IS SIMPLY A PSYCHOLOGICAL PARLOR TRICK - A SYMBOLIC "SHELL GAME"; HIS BRAND OF MAGIC AMOUNTING TO NOTHING MORE THAN AN ILLUSION CREATED TO FOOL THOSE UNEDUCATED SEARCHERS AND DIVORCE THEM OF THEIR MONEY. HIS LEGACY OF DECEPTION REMAINS STRONG AND MY COVEN BENEFITS GREATLY FROM THE IMPOTENCE OF THE CHURCH OF SATAN (AS WELL AS OTHER "CHURCHES").

ZEENA SCHRECK, LAVEY'S DAUGHTER, HAS OFTEN SPOKE AGAINST HER FATHER'S BELIEF (BETTER YET HIS NON-BELIEF). SHE CLAIMED HER FATHER WAS NOTHING MORE THAN A SHYSTER; A CONMAN; DOING NOTHING MORE THAN FOOLING THE UNEDUCATED IN HIS SHADOWY INTERPRETATION OF MAGIC[13].

ZEENA ALSO CLAIMS LAVEY WAS LAZY, UNMOTIVATED AND DID NOT TAKE RESPONSIBILITY FOR HIMSELF NOR HIS FAMILY. AS I EXPLAINED IN "VOLUME I: THE SATANIST", TAKING RESPONSIBILITY FOR A PERSON'S OWN ACTIONS IS SATANIC. IGNORING PERSONAL RESPONSIBILITY, IS NOT SATAN-

---

[13] http://www.vice.com/en_ca/read/beelzebubs-daughter-0000175-v19n4

IC BUT ATHEISTIC. SATANIST ARE RESPONSIBLE FOR THEIR ACTIONS.

THERE IS NEVER A TIME WHEN THE SATANIST SHOULD TURN AWAY FROM HIS / HER RESPONSIBIL-ITY. TO DO SO, IS NOT SATANIC! THE FRUIT OF SA-TANIC MAGIC COMES FROM TAKING RESPONSIBILI-TY.

TO KNOW SATAN IS TO LOVE SATAN; HE IS THE PRIMARY DRIVING FORCE BEHIND SATANIC MAGIC. SATAN AND HIS DEMONS ARE ALSO THE DRIVING FORCE BEHIND THE HIGHER SATANIC MAGIC PRO-CESSES AS I SPOKE ABOUT IN VOLUME I OF THIS SE-RIES. WITHOUT THE COMBINATION OF SATAN AND DEMONIC FAMILIARS, THERE IS NO SATANIC MAG-IC. WITH OUT THE ESSENCE OF SATANIC MAGIC, THOSE PROCESSES AND PROCEDURES NEEDED TO EN-SURE THE POSITIVE OUTCOME OF THE SATANIST'S DESIRES WILL NEVER BE MASTERED. WITHOUT THIS EDUCATION, A PERSON IS BLINDLY MUMBLING RITUALS THAT WILL BEAR NO FRUIT!

THERE ARE OFTEN THINGS IN A CHILD'S LIFE THAT LIFE ITSELF DESTROYS. INNOCENCE IS ONE THING THE WORLD CLEARLY, OVER TIME, DESTROYS. CHILD-LIKE INNOCENCE AND THE CHILD-LIKE UN-

DERSTANDING OF MAGIC, IS SLOWLY TAKEN AWAY THROUGH SYSTEMATIC RELIGIOUS AND / OR SOCIETAL ABUSES.

CHILDREN OFTEN KNOW MAGIC EXISTS AND THEY USE MAGIC, ALTHOUGH NOT FULLY AWARE OF THE ESSENCE, ELEMENTS OR POWERS. SOME TIME DURING DEVELOPMENT, THE PRECIOUS GIFT IS TAKEN FROM THE CHILD; WHETHER PARENTS RELENTLESSLY TELLING THE CHILD TO "STOP DOING SOMETHING" OR WHETHER THE CHILD ENTERS THE AGE WHERE ESTABLISHED RELIGION STIFLES THE CREATIVITY OF MAGIC; EITHER WAY, THAT PRECIOUS LINK WITH THE OTHER SIDE IS SLOWLY (AND IN SOME CASES FOREVER) DESTROYED.

IF YOU HAVE BEEN FORBIDDEN TO QUESTION A PRECEPT, THAT IS PROBABLY THE BEST TIME TO IN FACT, QUESTION THE VERY THING. MANY PEOPLE HAVE DIED AT THE HANDS OF "LEADERS" SIMPLY BECAUSE THEY WERE FORBIDDEN TO ASK QUESTIONS OR DISAGREE WITH A GURU, PRIEST, RABBI, PREACHER, ETC.

IT HAPPENS EVERY DAY AND EVEN THOUGH WE HAVE TECHNOLOGY AT OUR FINGERTIPS TWENTY-FOUR HOURS A DAY, WE HAVE ACTUALLY REGRESSED

WHEN IT COMES TO QUESTIONING BELIEFS AND BE-
LIEF SYSTEMS. WE (METAPHORICALLY) TAKE TWO
STEPS FORWARD AND FIVE STEPS BACKWARD. THE
DESIRE FOR A "QUICK FIX" OR "EASY WAY OUT" OF-
TEN BLINDS PEOPLE INTO <u>"SEEING WHAT THEY
WANT TO BELIEVE"</u>. TRAGEDY QUICKLY FOLLOWS.

THE SATANIST TAKES HER / HIS PLACE AMONG
THOSE PERSECUTED BEFORE AND WILL BE
AFTERWARD. IT IS AN HONOR HOWEVER, SUFFER
NOT. IF YOU ARE LEARNING AND PRACTICING
SATANIC MAGIC, YOU WILL ACQUIRE THE ABILITIES
TO TURN THE TABLES AND NO LONGER BE A
VICTIM.

HIC ET NUNC

PEOPLE OFTEN LOOK FOR VERY DIFFICULT AND CUMBERSOME SOLUTIONS TO THEIR PROBLEMS. THOSE WHO HAVE NOT STUDIED OCCULT ARTS OFTEN FIND THEMSELVES AT A DEAD END (METAPHORICALLY SPEAKING) BECAUSE THERE IS NOTHING THEY CAN DO TO CHANGE THE REALITY OF THEIR CIRCUMSTANCES. CHANGING REALITY IS A RESULT OF ACTIONS OF TRUE SATANISTS HOWEVER, THE 'MAGIC' COMES FROM SATAN. HE AND HIS DEMONS CHANGE THE REALITY MAGICALLY; A RESULT OF SYSTEMATIC APPLICATION OF SATANIC PROCESSES.

SATAN AND DEMONS EXIST IN A PARALLEL UNIVERSE; ONE DIMENSION REMOVED FROM THE THREE WE CAN PERCEIVE AND GRASP. I COVERED PARTS OF THIS IN VOLUME I OF THIS SERIES HOWEVER, IT DESERVES A WORD OR TWO HEREIN.

THE KNOWLEDGE AND APPLICATION OF THE TECHNIQUES NEEDED FOR SATANISTS TO COMMUNICATE WITH SATAN AND DEMONS IS MAGIC AND MAGICAL OPERATIONS. MAGICAL OPERATIONS WITHOUT COMMUNICATIONS = "NO ACTIONS".

SATAN DESIRES A RELATIONSHIP WITH THE TRUE SATANIST. THE VIRTUE OF A RELATIONSHIP IS TO FORM A WIN-WIN ARRANGEMENT WHEREIN ALL PARTIES REALIZE A MUTUAL BENEFIT. THOSE ATHEISTS WHO CALL THEMSELVES BY HIS NAME ARE DOING NOTHING MORE THAN BLASPHEMING THE MOST SATANIC.

SATAN IS 'UNDERSTANDING' OF HUMAN LIMITATIONS HOWEVER, SATAN HAS NEVER BEEN A HYPOCRITE! FOR THOSE WHO CLAIM TO BE SATANISTS YET DO NOT BELIEVE IN SATAN, THEY WILL EXPERIENCE HIS WRATH IN A PERPETUAL CYCLE OF FUTILITY AND SUFFERING.

THERE IS MUCH TO BE SAID ABOUT COMMUNICATION WITH THE DEVIL AND WITH THE LEGION OF DEMONS. I FEEL IT IS VERY IMPORTANT FOR THE READER TO FULLY UNDERSTAND AND APPRECIATE THE TECHNIQUES NEEDED TO RESULT IN A FORMAL, ITERATIVE COMMUNICATION CHANNEL WITHIN THE DIMENSIONS TRANSVERSED BY SATAN AND DEMONS.

THERE HAVE ALWAYS BEEN SKEPTICS WHEN IT COMES TO THE OCCULT ARTS; MORE ESPECIALLY BELIEVING IN THOSE THINGS THAT ARE BEYOND OUR

EARTHLY REALM. FOR SOME, THESE EXPERIENCES OF INVITING SATAN AND HIS DEMONS TO RITUALS MAY SEEM TO BE FAR-FETCHED. FOR SOME, THE BELIEF IN SUPERNATURAL THINGS MAY BE SIMPLY MORE THAN THEY CAN GRASP.

ONE THING THAT ALWAYS AMAZES ME IS THE FACT THAT SOMEONE WILL SHOUT "HAIL SATAN" HOWEVER, THEY DO NOT BELIEVE IN SATAN. FOR ME, SATANISM IS (HAS BEEN AND ALWAYS WILL BE) RESERVED FOR THE WORSHIP OF SATAN AND THE HOSTS OF HELL. IN MY OPINION, WHEN AN ATHEIST ATTACKS YOU FOR "WORSHIPING THE DEVIL" YOU WILL HAVE THE SATISFACTION OF KNOWING THEY HAVE "NO SATANIC STRENGTH IN THIS WORLD BEYOND THAT OF THEIR OWN PHYSICAL LIMITATIONS!!" LET ME SAY THAT AGAIN; TAKE COMFORT IN KNOWING ATHEISTS CANNOT BRING MAGIC NOR EFFECTIVE MAGICAL OPERATIONS AGAINST YOU (OR YOUR COVEN) FOR THEY ARE INCOMPETENT AND POWERLESS!!

SATAN, THE HOSTS OF HELL AND HIS ATTENDING COURT HAVE GIVEN US THE INFORMATION AND THE KNOWLEDGE TO PURSUE THOSE THINGS BEYOND OUR EARTHLY BOUNDARIES. YOU MUST REMAIN

OPEN-MINDED AND ASTUTELY SEEK TO LEARN, IM-PLEMENT, ASSESS, ACT AND RECTIFY THE AREAS OF YOUR LIFE WHICH WILL REQUIRE CHANGE.

IN THE FIRST OF THIS SERIES, I EXPLAINED HOW A SATANIST IN MODERN SOCIETY CAN BUILD A SOLID SATANIC FOUNDATION THAT IS STRONG ENOUGH TO WITHSTAND ATTACKS. WITHOUT THE STRONG FOUNDATION, THE SATANIST WILL "EXIST" IN A CONFINEMENT OF FEAR; FEAR IS NOT SATAN-IC, IN FACT, FEAR IS A HUMAN EMOTION WHICH HAS NO PLACE WITHIN THE SATANIC SANCTUM NOR DOES IT BELONG WITHIN THE CIRCLES OF THE SATANIC WITCHES' COVEN. FEAR IS BUT ONE OF THE HUMAN EMOTIONS THAT MUST BE OVERCOME IN ORDER TO BE SUCCESSFUL AS A SATANIC MAGI-CIAN.

TO FEAR IS TO LITERALLY PARALYZE ONESELF WITHOUT BEING ABLE TO MOVE AND HAVE FLEXI-BILITY TO COUNTER, MITIGATE AND / OR AVOID CERTAIN UNDESIRABLE CIRCUMSTANCES OR OUT-COMES. THOSE WHO CHOOSE NOT TO BELIEVE (OR DO NOT POSSESS THE COGNITIVE CAPACITY TO BELIEVE) HAVE, IN ESSENCE, RENDERED THEMSELVES IMPO-TENT........MAGICALLY SPEAKING.

WITHOUT THE DEMONS JUST BEYOND THE PAR-
ALLAX DIMENSION, THERE CAN BE NO REAL MAGIC
IN YOUR PURSUIT OF THE SATANIC HIGHER MAGIC
PROCESSES. YOU MUST ESTABLISH AND FORM A
STRONG FOUNDATION; FOR WITHOUT THE STRONG
FOUNDATION YOUR MAGIC WILL BE BASED UPON
NOTHING.

THESE PROCESSES ARE DEVELOPED OVER TIME
HOWEVER, ALL SYSTEMIC PROCESSES BEGIN WITH
ELEMENTARY MAGICAL OPERATIONS; 'RITUALS AND
SPELLS'. IN SATANISM, JUST AS WITCHCRAFT IN
GENERAL, THE SPIRIT WORLD MUST EFFECTIVELY
ASSIST THE PRACTITIONER HOWEVER, THE PRACTI-
TIONER MUST KNOW AND PRACTICE THE MAGIC
FOR WHICH THEY WILL USE. WITHOUT A HEALTHY
RESPECT FOR "WHERE THE MAGIC TRULY COMES
FROM" AND "WHO DELIVERS THE MAGICAL
DESIRES", NO BASIC PROCESSES CAN BE MASTERED.

IF YOU DO NOT BELIEVE IN THE EXISTENCE OF
SATAN, YOU ARE WASTING YOUR TIME READING
THIS BOOK. IF YOU FEEL THERE IS NO SATANIC
BODY (CORPUS SATANAS) BEYOND OUR REALM,
YOU SHOULD STOP NOW AND NOT WASTE YOUR
TIME; FOR WHAT I AM ABOUT TO SHARE IS EITHER

GOING TO LEAD TO A POSITIVE CHANGE IN YOUR BEHAVIOR OR WILL END BADLY FOR YOU. IT WILL EITHER LEAVE A POSITIVE INFLUENCE ON YOUR PSYCHE OR YOU WILL SIMPLY END UP MOCKING EVERYTHING THAT I EXPLAIN IN THIS SERIES. DO NOT MOCK SATAN......FOR TO DO SO WILL CERTAINLY BRING THE WRATH OF THE DEVIL AND HIS COURT UPON YOU.

WHEN WE WERE CHILDREN, WE OFTEN HAD MAGICAL EXPERIENCES. AS WE GREW OLDER, WE WERE TAUGHT THESE THINGS EITHER 1) DID NOT HAPPEN OR 2) THEY WERE NOT REAL. WE WERE TOLD THESE THINGS WERE "OUR IMAGINATIONS" AND BECAUSE OF THAT, WE INDIVIDUALLY FORMED A CALLOUS OVER THE MAGICAL MIND.

BECAUSE OF RIDICULE THAT PERHAPS YOUR PARENTS, YOUR RELATIVES OR FRIENDS HEAPED UPON YOU, THOSE THOUGHTS, MEMORIES AND EXPERIENCES HAVE BEEN SUPPRESSED DEEP WITH IN YOUR SUBCONSCIOUS. THERE HAVE BEEN NO CHANGES IN THE SPIRITUAL WORLD; YOU SIMPLY HAVE CHANGED THE WAY YOU PERCEIVE THAT WORLD.

EARLY ON, DO YOU REMEMBER A TIME WHEN YOU HAD A SPECIAL FRIEND WHO WOULD COME

AND VISIT YOU AT NIGHT? PERHAPS THIS FRIEND WAS AN APPARITION OR PERHAPS A GHOST; PERHAPS IT SEEMED LIKE A DEMON BUT AS TIME WENT ON AND YOU GREW OLDER, YOU PROBABLY, LIKE MANY OTHERS, FORCED THOSE FEELINGS DEEP DOWN INSIDE. TO TALK ABOUT SUCH THINGS WOULD BE A SIN IN A 'CHRISTIAN HOME'; TO SPEAK OF SUCH OCCURRENCES WOULD MAKE YOU SOUND "CRAZY" AROUND YOUR FRIENDS; EVEN WHISPERING ABOUT SUCH AN OCCURRENCE WOULD CAUSE YOUR CLASSMATES TO MAKE FUN OF YOU AND CALL YOU NAMES. THIS MAY ACTUALLY CONTINUE TO HAPPEN TODAY IN SOME CAPACITY.

FOR THOSE OF US WHO EXPERIENCE SATANIC MAGIC, WE HAVE LEARNED TO DEAL WITH SUCH CIRCUMSTANCES. BECAUSE ANOTHER PERSON HAS NOT EXPERIENCED OR UNLOCKED THE SECRETS OF MAGIC, DOES NOT MEAN HE / SHE CANNOT; IT SIMPLY MEANS HE / SHE MAY BE TOO LAZY OR CLOSED-MINDED TO PURSUE SUCH GREAT THINGS.

FOR OVER 25 YEARS, I HAVE BEEN SATANICALLY ACTIVE AND HAVE RECEIVED "GREAT REWARDS" FOR DOING SO. THE LAWS OF PHYSICS, MATHEMATICS, ALCHEMY AND MANY OTHER SCIENCES ARE NOT

TO BE IGNORED SINCE THEY TOO HAVE A PLACE IN MAGIC. FOR INSTANCE, IF YOU ARE PREPARING A CERTAIN ELIXIR FOR A RITUAL, YOU WILL CERTAINLY USE SCIENCE AND PERHAPS CHEMISTRY TOGETHER.

REMEMBER, NOT SO MANY YEARS AGO, HUMANS THOUGHT THE WORLD WAS FLAT! WE ALSO DID NOT BELIEVE IN GRAVITY, THE SCIENCES OF PROPULSION OR PHYSICS.....SUCH AS INERTIA. WE CANNOT SEE THE WIND AND YET IT CARRIES THINGS IN A MOLECULAR FASHION, DEMONSTRATING GREAT POWER. WE HAVE NOT FULLY HARNESSED THE WIND BUT, CLAIMING THE WIND DOES NOT EXIST SIMPLY BECAUSE YOU DO NOT SEE IT, IS TO TURN A BLIND EYE TO A PRINCIPLE THAT IS KNOWN; OF WHICH THE EFFECTS CAN BE CLEARLY SEEN.

THE SAME APPLIES IN MAGIC. JUST BECAUSE A LIGHTNING BOLT CANNOT BE HARNESSED, DOES NOT MEAN WE SHOULD DISREGARD ITS AWESOME POWER! WE CAN SEE IT AND WE CAN HEAR THE SUDDEN EXPANSION AND CONTRACTION OF THE AIR AS THE LIGHT MOVES AT LIGHT SPEED HOWEVER, WE CAN'T HARNESS THE ENERGY NOR CAN WE SAMPLE ITS AWESOME POWER. TO DO SO WOULD MEAN CERTAIN

DEATH.

FOR THOSE OF US WHO HAVE BEEN IN THE WORLD OF MAGIC FOR QUITE SOME TIME, THERE ARE SOME THINGS THAT ARE JUST AS POWERFUL, IF NOT MORE POWERFUL, THAN THE BOLT OF LIGHTNING. FOR THIS REASON, YOU MUST PREPARE, PRACTICE, STUDY AND LEARN BEFORE YOU ATTEMPT TO HARNESS SUCH ENERGY WHICH COULD VERY EASILY TAKE YOUR LIFE.

INVOCANDUM

SATANIC SPIRITS EXIST AS SPHERE-LIKE 'ORBS'; THE ENERGY DISPLACEMENT OF SPACE AND TIME. WHEN A SPIRIT FIRST APPEARS TO A PRACTITIONER, ESPECIALLY A NEW PRACTITIONER OF THE MAGICAL ARTS, HE / SHE WILL ALMOST CERTAINLY BEGIN TO QUESTION IF THEY ARE REALLY SEEING WHAT THEY BELIEVE THEY SEE. THE DEMONIC WORLD IS SO DIF-FERENT (AND MORE ADVANCED) THAN OUR PHYS-ICAL HUMAN REALITY. IT IS ALMOST CERTAIN AF-TER THE FIRST MANIFESTATION OF A DEMON, THE PRACTITIONER WILL ATTEMPT TO COMPLETELY TALK HIM / HERSELF OUT OF BELIEF IN THE EVENT.

THERE ARE THOSE WHO I HAVE SPOKEN WITH WHO HAVE TRIED TO EXPLAIN (DISMISS) THE MANI-FESTATION AS AN EFFECT OF "DRUGS OR ALCOHOL". I SIMPLY SMILE BECAUSE I KNOW BY WHAT THEY ARE DESCRIBING, THE EVENT TRULY OCCURRED; THE SEQUENCE OF EVENTS LEADING UP TO AN ACTUAL APPEARANCE OF A DEMON. IT IS ALMOST ALWAYS THE SAME LOGICAL CHAIN OF EVENTS EVERY TIME.

BY HEARING CERTAIN KEYWORDS IN THE EX-PLANATION, I CAN ALMOST UNEQUIVOCALLY

GUARANTEE THAT THE MANIFESTATION OF THE DEMON DID HAPPEN AND NOTHING ELSE NEEDS TO BE SAID. THOSE WHO HAVE EXPERIENCED MANIFESTATIONS, ESPECIALLY NEW PRACTITIONERS, ARE ALMOST "ASHAMED OR EMBARRASSED" TO MENTION THE EVENT AND THIS IS QUITE UNDERSTANDABLE.

EXPLAINING THE EVENT TO SOMEONE WHO HAS NEVER EXPERIENCED IT IS ALMOST LIKE EXPLAINING WHAT A "FLYING SAUCER LANDING IN YOUR YARD" LOOKS LIKE. I CAN ATTEST TO THE FACT THAT DEMONS EXIST, SATAN EXISTS AND THEY REGULARLY MANIFEST THEMSELVES WHEN SUMMONED IN THE CORRECT MANNER.

THERE ARE MANY WHO PROVIDE LIES FOR THE POPULATION TO CONSUME. THERE ARE THOSE WHO GLADLY TAKE YOUR MONEY, TIME AND PERHAPS EVEN 'MORE' AND SELL YOU LIES. SATAN DOES NOT WANT THAT FOR YOU. HE WANTS YOU TO KNOW THE TRUTH IF YOU ARE WILLING TO ACCEPT THE TRUTH. IT MAY TAKE SOME TIME TO "UNLEARN" SOME OF THE LIES. IT SIMPLY TAKES TIME FOR A PERSON TO FREE THEMSELVES FROM THE CHAINS OF LIES.

I WAS THE PRODUCT OF A BROKEN HOME WHERE I WAS SUBJECTED TO COUNTLESS SITUATIONS WHICH MADE ME FEEL INADEQUATE, FOOLISH AND UNCOMFORTABLE. I WAS ABUSED (VERBALLY AND PHYSICALLY) BY A MOTHER WHO WOULD CALL UPON HER GOD WHILE PROCEEDING TO BEAT ME. I WAS BELITTLED, VERBALLY AND PSYCHOLOGICALLY ABUSED AND MADE TO BELIEVE MY LIFE WAS WORTHLESS. IT TOOK YEARS TO "UNLEARN" THOSE LIES AND MY PROGRAMMING. I HAD BEEN SYSTEMATIC BRAINWASHED.

GIVEN TIME, A PERSON MAY ACTUALLY TALK THEMSELVES INTO SEEING WHAT IS NOT REAL. THEY MAY ALSO TALK THEMSELVES OUT OF SEEING WHAT IS TRULY REAL JUST BECAUSE THEY CHOOSE NOT TO BELIEVE.

PEOPLE CAN EASILY TALK THEMSELVES OUT OF THE TRUTH. I SEE IT MANY TIMES AND I HEAR IT IN COUNTLESS CONVERSATIONS. THOSE WHO ARE SEEKING THE TRUTH SIMPLY OVERLOOK THE TRUTH BECAUSE THEY DO NOT WANT TO ACCEPT REALITY AS IT IS. YOU MUST ACCEPT YOUR REALITY IN ORDER TO CHANGE YOUR REALITY. LYING TO YOURSELF HURTS YOU MORE THAN ANYONE ELSE. WHY

LIE TO YOURSELF? ACCEPT REALITY AND SEE THINGS FOR WHAT THEY TRULY REPRESENT. EMBRACE REALITY AND CHANGE IT IF YOU SO DESIRE.

OVER THE LAST 25+ YEARS I HAVE EXPERIMENTED AND LEARNED FROM THOSE THINGS REVEALED THROUGH MY DILIGENT PRACTICE AND PURSUIT OF SATANIC KNOWLEDGE. THOSE WHO ARE NOT INVESTING IN THEMSELVES ARE SIMPLY INVESTING IN SOMEONE ELSE, FOR THERE WILL ONLY BE THOSE WHO KNOW AND THOSE WHO ARE WAITING FOR ANSWERS TO BE SPOON-FED TO THEM.

NOTHING IS FREE; EVERYTHING COSTS AND KNOWLEDGE IS NO DIFFERENT. EVEN IF YOUR TUITION IS PAID 100% AT THE MOST PRESTIGIOUS OF UNIVERSITIES, YOU MUST ATTEND CLASSES, WORK AND MAKE THE GRADES TO RECEIVE A DEGREE.

THERE ARE THOSE HOWEVER, WHO WILL CHOOSE TO WASTE WHAT HAS BEEN GIVEN TO THEM. EVEN IF EVERYTHING IS 100% PAID, THEY WILL STILL FIND AN EXCUSE WHY THEY CANNOT COMPLETE THE MOST SIMPLE OF TASKS NEEDED TO SUCCEED. THESE INDIVIDUALS THINK THEY ARE 'GETTING BY WITH SOMETHING'; THEY THINK THEY ARE BENEFITING FROM THE STUPIDITY OF OTHERS.

THERE ARE THOSE WHO WILL LIE TO YOUR FACE BUT YOU SHOULD NOT LIE TO YOURSELF. EVALUATE AND ACCEPT EVERY SITUATION FOR WHAT IT TRULY IS. YOU MAY OR MAY NOT BE A VICTIM HOWEVER, THAT DOES NOT CHANGE THE FACT YOU HAVE THE POWER TO CHANGE YOUR FUTURE AND YOU MUST MAKE SOME ADJUSTMENTS IN COURSE TO ARRIVE AT YOUR PLANNED DESTINATION.

IF YOU HAVE NOT SET A COURSE, YOU WILL NEVER KNOW WHEN YOU ARRIVE AND AS SUCH, NO DESTINATION WILL BE THE "RIGHT DESTINATION". MANY PEOPLE DO NOT KNOW 'WHERE THEY WANT TO BE IN LIFE' AND WITHOUT PLANNING, THEY WILL NOT SUCCEED.....IT'S REALLY THAT SIMPLE.

THERE ARE THOSE WHO WILL JUDGE YOU AND PERHAPS CHASTISE YOU FOR WHAT YOU BELIEVE. UNDERSTAND THIS IS PERFECTLY NATURAL AND BECAUSE YOU CHOOSE TO BECOME A SATANIST, DOES NOT MEAN THE WORLD WILL CEASE TO TREAT YOU THE WAY IT HAS IN THE PAST. JUST BECAUSE YOU CHANGE YOUR ACTIONS DOES NOT MEAN THE WORLD WILL CHANGE AS WELL. YOU MUST CHANGE YOUR REALITY AND THE WORLD WILL

CHANGE AS A RESULT.

BECOMING A SATANIST SIMPLY MEANS YOU HAVE DECIDED TO CHANGE THE WAY "YOU PERCEIVE THE WORLD" AND THE WAY YOU PROCESS THE INFORMATION YOU RECEIVE THROUGH YOUR SENSES. BECOMING A SATANIST WILL BUILD STRONG CHARACTER AND PROVIDE FAITH IN YOUR CAPABILITIES.

NOT EVERYONE IS READY TO MAKE THE CHANGES REQUIRED IN ORDER TO CHANGE PERCEPTION AND ULTIMATELY CHANGE THEIR REALITY. TAKE MY WORDS OF TRUTH......FOR I SHARE THEM WITH YOU AS A FRIEND; I WANT YOU TO SUCCEED! SATAN WANTS YOU TO SUCCEED!

THE FIRST TIME YOU EXPERIENCE A MANIFESTATION OF A DEMON OR PERHAPS THE LORD SATAN HIMSELF, YOU ARE GOING TO QUESTION EVERYTHING YOU HAVE BELIEVED IN THE PAST. IF YOU DO NOT CHANGE YOUR MIND, YOUR REALITY WILL NEVER CHANGE. WHY DO YOU THINK SOME PEOPLE ARE 'MILLIONAIRES' AND ARE SO UNHAPPY?

YOU MAY THINK "IF I HAD MILLIONS OF DOLLARS, I WOULD BE HAPPY BECAUSE I COULD BUY

ANYTHING I WANTED!!" EXTERNAL FACTORS DO NOT CAUSE HAPPINESS; TEMPORARY DISTRACTIONS PERHAPS HOWEVER, NEVER HAPPINESS...EVER. HAPPINESS AND FULFILLMENT BEGINS AND ENDS WITHIN ONESELF.

JABEL MUNTAR

"THE ROAD OF GOOD INTENTIONS IS PAVED WITH TEARS; THE WAY TO NOWHERE."

ALEISTER NACHT

WE MAY INTEND TO DO OUR VERY BEST IN LIFE. I DO NOT BELIEVE ANYONE SETS OUT TO IN-TENTIONALLY FAIL HOWEVER, AS THE OLD SAYING GOES; "NO ONE PLANS TO FAIL, THEY SIMPLY FAIL TO PLAN."

THE SAME CAN BE SAID FOR SATANISM. THOSE WHO ARE DILIGENT AND PERFORM THEIR 'DUE DILI-GENCE' WILL BE REWARDED GREATLY IN RETURN. JUST AS A FARMER PLANTS A FIELD AND EXPECTS A RETURN ON HIS TIME AND INVESTMENT, SO SHOULD YOU EXPECT A RETURN ON YOUR IN-VESTMENT OF TIME AND MONEY AS YOU PURSUE MAGICAL PERFECTION.

AS HUMANS, WE MUST EXPERIENCE THINGS IN ORDER TO LEARN. THIS IS WHY WE ATTEND A UNI-

VERSITY, TAKE CLASSES AND COURSES TO LEARN EITHER A PROFESSION OR A VOCATIONAL / TECHNICAL TRADE. WITHOUT EXPERIENCING THESE EVENTS, WE WILL NEVER LEARN OR ACQUIRE THE SKILLS NEEDED TO EARN A LIVING AND ACHIEVE THOSE THINGS WE ASPIRE. THERE IS NO SUCH THING AS "SPONTANEOUS KNOWLEDGE" FOR THE HUMAN. ALL WE KNOW (AND WILL EVER KNOW) IS WHAT WE LEARN THROUGH ABSTRACT, THEORETICAL, OR PRACTICAL LEARNING EXPERIENCES.

AS I EXPERIMENTED WITH DIFFERENT RITUALS AND AS I LEARNED MORE AND MORE FROM MY 'MATERNAL' VOODOO / HOODOO SPONSORS, I BEGAN TO BLOSSOM, UNDERSTAND AND UNLOCK THOSE SECRETS THAT HAD BEEN THERE ALL ALONG. I COULD NEITHER SEE THEM NOR UNDERSTAND THEIR MEANINGS UNTIL THE TIME WAS RIGHT; MEANING I HAD REACHED A POINT WHERE THERE WAS MEANING.....A MEANING I COULD GRASP AND UNDERSTAND. YOU MUST, AND I REPEAT YOU MUST, CLEAR YOUR MIND OF ALL CHAOS, PAIN, WORRY AND TROUBLE IN ORDER TO UNLOCK THE SECRETS OF MAGIC.

MAGIC ITSELF COMES FROM PEACEFUL STATES OF

SOLITUDE AND INTERLUDES OF REFLECTION AND TRANQUILITY WITHIN THE MIND. SATANIC MEDITATION IS A FORM OF PEACEFUL INTERCONNECTION WITHIN THE REALM OF BODY, MIND AND SPIRIT. THE CHAKRAS OPEN AND ENERGY FLOWS FREELY INTO THE CHASM; THE AREA WHERE IT IS NEEDED IN ORDER TO PRODUCE THE DESIRES OF ONE'S HEART. THE FOLLOWING BLOG POST EXCERPT (SATANIC MAGIC BLOG) EXPLAINS THIS CONCEPT FAIRLY WELL:

"THE HEART PLAYS A KEY ROLE IN MANY OF THE BODY'S BIOLOGICAL FUNCTIONS WHILE SERVING VITAL ROLES IN THE EMOTIONAL SYSTEM AND SUBSYSTEMS OF A PERSON'S LIFE. THE HEART ALSO UTILIZES SMALL ELECTRICAL CURRENTS WHICH NOT ONLY SEND THE SIGNAL TO THE HEART TO "BEAT" BUT IT ALSO SETS THE APPROPRIATE RHYTHM NEEDED TO ENSURE THE NEEDS OF THE BODY ARE MET, WHETHER SITTING ON THE SOFA OR JOGGING DOWN A SIDEWALK. IT IS IRONIC AND TERRIFYING AT THE SAME TIME TO REALIZE WE ARE ALL ONE HEARTBEAT AWAY FROM DEATH. THAT FACT IS VERY HARD FOR SOME PEOPLE TO HANDLE HOWEVER, THE SATANIST

VIEWS THIS PHILOSOPHICAL "EDGE OF THE CLIFF" AS JUST ANOTHER EVENT THAT OCCURS DAILY IN THE ANIMAL KINGDOM."

MAGUS ALEISTER NACHT

SATANISM AND YOUR CHAKRAS — PART 4

YOU CANNOT ACHIEVE THAT REALM; YOU CANNOT ACHIEVE THAT STATE OF 'HIGHER AWARENESS' WITHOUT CLEARING YOUR CHAKRAS. TO CLEAR THE CHAKRAS, YOU MUST CLEAR YOUR MIND, OPEN YOUR SPIRIT, BODY AND OVERALL SYSTEM AND ACCEPT THE ENERGIES THAT WILL FLOW FREELY THROUGH YOUR BODY, JUST AS BLOOD FLOWS FREELY THROUGH YOUR VEINS.

WITHIN AN ENVIRONMENT OF CONSTANT CHAOS AND CEASELESS HEARTACHE, IT REQUIRES INCREASINGLY MORE ENERGY 'SIMPLY TO EXIST' WHEN YOU ARE IN THE STORM. IT BECOMES MORE DIFFICULT FOR YOU TO REMOVE DISTRACTIONS AND BREAK THE CHAINS OF SYMBOLIC SLAVERY. YOU BEGIN TO LIE AND CHEAT YOURSELF OF HAPPINESS; ATTEMPTING TO JUSTIFY THE REASONING,

ALMOST VOLLEYING BOTH POSITIVE AND NEGATIVE SIDES OF "TORTUROUS SELF PROTECTION / SELF LOATHING DUALITY". MEANWHILE, THE LIFE YOU DESPERATELY WANTED FADES INTO OBLIVION AND ALL IS (PERCEIVED AS) LOST.

THE SATANIC MEDITATIONS I USE ARE DERIVATIVES OF QUIET MEDITATIONS FROM THE PRACTICE OF HOODOO. THERE IS NO BETTER WAY TO PREPARE YOURSELF FOR A RITUAL OR JOURNEY ON THE ASTRAL PLANE. IF YOU HARNESS YOUR ENERGY AND CALM YOUR DEMONS, YOU WILL FIND A PEACEFUL PREPARATION ENVIRONMENT HOWEVER, YOU MUST MAKE A COMMITMENT TO YOURSELF AND YOU MUST FULFILL THAT COMMITMENT.

SPEAKING OF COMMITMENT, SO MANY PEOPLE WANT THE BLESSINGS OF SATAN AND THE REWARDS OF MAGIC HOWEVER, THEY ARE AFRAID TO MAKE A COMMITMENT! PERHAPS THEY DO NOT KNOW 'HOW TO PROPERLY MAKE A COMMITMENT' HOWEVER, WHERE THERE IS A WILL, THERE IS ALWAYS A WAY. THOSE WHO SEEK KNOWLEDGE AND POWER WILL FIND THEY MUST MAKE A COMMITMENT. IF YOU WANT TO BECOME AN ATTORNEY, ROCK STAR, BILLIONAIRE, SURGEON, ETC. YOU MUST MAKE A

111

COMMITMENT. YOU MUST CREATE A REALISTIC PLAN OF ACTION AND COMMIT YOURSELF <u>DAILY</u> TO ACHIEVING THAT WHICH YOU DESIRE. SUCCESS DOES NOT "JUST HAPPEN" BY CHANCE. "OH, DID YOU THINK BUYING THIS BOOK AND PERHAPS 'SELLING YOUR SOUL' WAS GOING TO MAKE YOU WEALTHY AND WILDLY SUCCESSFUL? YOU ARE LOOKING FOR 'DISNEYLAND'.

SUCCESS COMES FROM THE INTELLIGENTLY PLANNED ACTIVITIES AND STRONGLY COMMITTED ACTIONS THAT PRODUCE TANGIBLE, DESIRED RE-SULTS. WHETHER YOU WANT TO BE A RECORDING ARTIST OR WIN THE NOBEL PEACE PRIZE, IT BEGINS WITH A PLAN AND EFFORT OR THERE WILL BE NO SUCCESSFUL RESULTS.

THERE ARE ORDERS AND HIERARCHIES IN THE DEMONIC WORLD JUST AS THERE ARE ESTABLISHED HIERARCHIES IN OUR EARTHLY REALM. OUR WORLD HAS THREE DIMENSIONS BUT ON THE OTHER SIDE, THERE ARE MULTIPLE DIMENSIONS. OUR HUMAN PERCEPTION AND LOGIC MAKE IT DIFFICULT TO WRAP OUR MINDS AROUND SOME OF THE PRECEPTS OF THE OTHER SIDE, WHICH PRESENTS A CHALLENGE TO THE NEW PRACTITIONER.

DURING THE MONTH OF OCTOBER, THE VEIL SEPARATING OUR DIMENSIONS FROM THE OTHER DIMENSIONS BECOMES VERY THIN. THROUGHOUT RECORDED HISTORY, HUMANS HAVE LEARNED ABOUT THIS PHENOMENA WHICH "THINS THE VEIL". DURING THIS TIME, IT BECOMES VERY EASY TO ESTABLISH COMMUNICATION WITH THE OTHER SIDE; "THE DEMONIC WORLD". FOR THIS REASON, COMMUNICATIONS, RITUALS, SÉANCES, MAGICAL OPERATIONS AND OTHER OCCULT WORKINGS ACHIEVE MUCH BETTER (MORE SUCCESSFUL) RE-SULTS DURING THIS TIME OF EACH YEAR.

THE ABILITY OF HUMANS TO COMMUNICATE WITH THOSE WHO HAVE 'GONE BEFORE' IS NOTHING NEW. THIS MAGICAL OPERATION HAS BEEN AROUND FOR YEARS AND YEARS. SOME OPERATIONS HAVE BEEN CALLED 'HOLY' BY ESTABLISHED RELIGIONS AND CALLED 'UNHOLY' BY THE SAME. WHATEVER THE NAME OR DEFINITION, THERE ARE THOSE WHO CAN EASILY COMMUNICATE WITH THE OTHER SIDE.

ONE WHO IS 'ON THE OTHER SIDE' IS SATAN HIMSELF. HE HAS RICHLY INVESTED AND REVEALED KNOWLEDGE THROUGHOUT HISTORY. I HAVE PER-SONALLY LEARNED MANY, MANY THINGS

THROUGH THE RELENTLESS PURSUIT OF STUDYING SATANISM. SATAN HAS REVEALED MANY THINGS TO ME AS A REWARD FOR MY RELENTLESSNESS, DILIGENCE AND DEDICATION TO LEARN MORE ABOUT HIM AND THE ANCIENT SECRETS OF MAGICAL WISDOM. THOSE WHO ARE WILLING AND ABLE TO "GO THE DISTANCE" BY LEARNING THOSE THINGS REQUIRED, CAN CULTIVATE AND DEVELOP ABILITIES ENABLING THEM TO 'COMMUNICATE AT WILL' WITH SATAN, THE CROWN PRINCES OF HELL, DEMONS, TEUTONIC SPIRITS AND THE HIERARCHY OF HELL; FROM TOP TO BOTTOM, GATE TO GATE.

CADUCEUS

DURING MY TEENAGE YEARS, I HAD SOME FRIGHTENING, HORRENDOUS AND PAINFUL THINGS OCCUR IN MY LIFE. ONE WAS WHEN I TRIED HEROIN. HEROIN REQUIRES ONLY ONE DOSE TO ALWAYS REMEMBER HOW GOOD (SHE) IT FEELS. HEROIN WAS BETTER THAN SEX; IT WAS BETTER THAN LIFE, I WOULD HAVE GLADLY GIVEN MY LIFE FOR ANOTHER NEEDLE BENEATH MY SKIN.

IT SOUNDS ALMOST ABSURD NOW BUT YEARS LATER, I HAVE GROWN, MATURED AND DEVELOPED AS A PERSON YET, I STILL REMEMBER HEROIN. SHE COULD EASILY TAKE MY LIFE AND IF I EVER ALLOWED HER INSIDE MY BODY AGAIN, SHE PROBABLY WILL SUCCEED AT KILLING ME. I KNOW THAT AND I GREATLY RESPECT THAT; SHE IS MY LIMITATION; SHE WILL NEVER BE MY LOVER AGAIN. AS CLINT EASTWOOD SAID "A MAN'S GOT TO KNOW HIS LIMITATIONS"!![14]

FOR ME, THERE WAS LIFE AFTER XTIANITY, AFTER BEING MENTALLY AND PHYSICALLY ABUSED AND AFTER BECOMING A SLAVE TO A NEEDLE FILLED

---

[14] _Magnum Force_ motion picture

WITH POISON. "TRUTH" REALLY DID SET ME FREE BECAUSE TRUTH WAS EXACTLY WHAT I FOUND - IT TOOK YEARS FOR ME TO FIND IT!

HAPPINESS WAS ALWAYS AN ELUSIVE CONCEPT FOR ME. I REMEMBER AS A YOUNG MAN IN NEW ORLEANS, THE MIDDLE OF THE NIGHT, SEARCHING FOR A DEALER WHO WOULD SELL ME ONE MORE FIX, ONE FINAL PUSH; MY TRIP TO THE TOP! SATAN WAS WITH ME DURING THOSE DAYS AND HE SHOWED ME TRUTH IN ONE OF THE MOST 'UNLIKELY OF PLACES' ON THE FACE OF THE EARTH.

THERE I WAS; A WHITE BOY IN THE LOWER NINTH WARD IN NEW ORLEANS, A BATTLEGROUND UNTO ITSELF AND I BELIEVE A CERTAIN PERSON WAS SENT TO CROSS MY PATH AND SAVE MY LIFE. SHE WAS A PRACTITIONER OF HOODOO AND I WILL NEVER FORGET THE FIRST WORDS SHE SAID TO ME AND I QUOTE; "SUGAR, YOU LOOKING FOR A PLACE TO DIE?" I SMILED BRUSH BACK MY LONG HAIR AND SAID "YES, I AM, AS A MATTER OF FACT. I'M ALREADY DEAD SO IT DOES NOT REALLY MATTER!"

SHE LAUGHED AND WE BECAME VERY CLOSE FRIENDS. SHE SHOWED ME SO MANY THINGS IN MAGIC BUT MORE THAN ANYTHING, I WILL AL-

WAYS THANK HER FOR SHOWING ME TRUTH AND SHOWING ME THERE IS A WAY THROUGH THE STORM AS OPPOSED TO STAYING IN THE STORM. THAT WAS THE PROBLEM WITH MY LIFE UP UNTIL THAT POINT. I WAS "IN THE STORM" AND THE STORM WAS WHERE I WANTED TO BE.

UNCONSCIOUSLY, I HAD BEEN TOLD AND PRO-GRAMMED TO STAY IN THE STORM ALL THE TIME. THERE WAS ALWAYS SOMETHING IN MY LIFE THAT WAS CAUSING DISPLEASURE AND PAIN. I BLED SO MANY TIMES FOR NOTHING; JUST BECAUSE I WAS LOOKING FOR THE EVER-ELUSIVE HAPPINESS AND TRUTH.

I BEGAN LEARNING AND PRACTICING HOODOO. I DELVED FURTHER INTO THE OCCULT ARTS. AS I BE-CAME CLEAN AND SOBER, MY MIND BEGAN TO OPEN UP. I WAS READY TO LEARN AND EXPERI-MENTED WITH DIFFERENT MAGICAL WORKINGS. I ACTUALLY FOUND THAT THE 'RECEPTIVE MIND' WHEN READY TO LEARN COULD BE EASILY CULTI-VATED TO GROW A BOUNTIFUL HARVEST OF KNOWLEDGE. HOODOO OPENED SEVERAL DOORS THAT LED ME TO SATANISM. ONE OF THE COMMON THEMES BETWEEN THE TWO OCCULT ARTS IS MAGI-

CAL OPERATIONS AND THE KNOWLEDGE AND ABILI-
TY TO MAGICALLY MANIPULATE THOSE THINGS IN
OUR DIMENSIONS IN ORDER TO ACHIEVE ONE'S DE-
SIRES.

SATAN BROUGHT THE FIRST OPEN KNOWLEDGE
TO HUMANS. SATAN DOES NOT WISH FOR YOU TO
LIVE IN THE DARK. YOU HAVE THE ABILITY TO
REACH OUT AND FORM A BRIDGE; A STRONG AL-
LIANCE AND RELATIONSHIP WITH SATAN. HE WILL
NOT LIE; HE TELLS THE TRUTH AND HE WILL LEAD
YOU TO THE TRUTH, IF YOU DILIGENTLY PURSUE
TRUTH.

THE PROBLEM IN OUR WORLD IS MANY PEOPLE
DO NOT WANT TO KNOW THE TRUTH SO THEY SIM-
PLY DISREGARD THAT WHICH SATAN FREELY OFFERS
AND THEY CHOOSE TO BELIEVE THE LIES THAT HAVE
BEEN CREATED BY THE ESTABLISHED CHURCH. THOSE
WHO CANNOT OR WILL NOT THINK FOR THEM-
SELVES WILL INDELIBLY BE MADE A PRISONER OF
THEIR OWN LACK OF KNOWLEDGE. SATAN WANTS
YOU TO KNOW THE TRUTH AND HE HAS SENT FA-
MILIARS INTO OUR REALM TO HELP ASSIST US WITH
MAKING INITIAL CONTACT AND WITH FORMING A
LASTING RELATIONSHIP WITH THE OTHER SIDE, IF WE

CHOOSE TO.

ANYONE CAN REACH OUT AND FIND THE KNOWLEDGE AND WISDOM. NO ONE WANTS TO LIVE IN IGNORANCE OR SHOULD I SAY "THERE ARE THOSE WHO WANT TO LIVE IN IGNORANCE AND FOR THAT REASON, THEY WILL BE FOREVER IGNORANT!" SOME SIMPLY CHOOSE TO DISREGARD TRUTH AND LIVE A PERPETUAL LIFE OF LIES. FOR SOME, A LIE IS EASIER TO LIVE WITH THAN THEIR TRUE REALITY.

SANCTUM OF SHADOWS CORPUS SATANAS

ALCHIMIA OMNI LIBER METU

THE KID WHO MIMICS A SATANIC RITUAL BY
RECITING THINGS THAT HE OR SHE HEARD, PERHAPS
IN A VIDEO, ON TELEVISION OR A MOVIE MAY AC-
TUALLY CROSS PATHS WITH A DEMON OR OTHER SU-
PERNATURAL BEING. MAGIC AND RITUAL ARE JUST
LIKE A KNIFE; IN CAPABLE HANDS, A KNIFE CAN
BE USED WITH PRECISION. FOR EXAMPLE, IN A DOC-
TOR'S HAND, A SCALPEL CAN REMOVE FLESH AND
TISSUE; IN THE HAND OF A CHILD, A SCALPEL MAY
VERY WELL INJURE OR KILL THE CHILD OR ANYONE
ELSE.

IT IS IMPORTANT TO VISUALIZE MAGIC. THE
PRACTITIONER WHO KNOWS WHAT MAGIC CAN DO
WILL CALL UPON THE FORCES OF DARKNESS AND
MANIPULATE THE ENERGY. BY WORKING WITH A
DEMON, THE PRACTITIONER CALLS FOR A CHANGE
IN REALITY TO OCCUR. FOR THE INCOMPETENT IN-
DIVIDUAL (I.E. DABBLER), MAGIC AND THE SUM-
MONING OF A SATANIC BEING MAY CAUSE THE
INDIVIDUAL'S INJURY AND / OR DEATH. IN
MANY CASES, THOSE WHO DO NOT KNOW WHAT
THEY ARE DOING WILL ATTEMPT TO SUMMON SA-

TAN HIMSELF; QUITE OFTEN TO THEIR DETRIMENT.

ANOTHER DANGER TO THE INEXPERIENCED, IN-
COMPETENT DABBLER IS THE SUMMONING OF A
DEMON SUCH IS AS AZAZEL OR SAMAEL. THESE
DEMONS ARE BENEFICIAL DURING DESTRUCTION
RITUALS AND THEY SERVE A GREAT PURPOSE AND
CONTRIBUTE A VALUE TO A RITUAL OPERATION.
ONE THING IS FOR SURE; IF THE MAGICIAN IS IN-
EXPERIENCED, THE RESULT WILL SURELY BE, AT THE
LEAST, A PAINFUL, FRIGHTENING AND UNPLEAS-
ANT EXPERIENCE. A PERSON THAT DOES NOT KNOW
HOW TO USE A WEAPON SHOULD NOT PLAY WITH
THE WEAPON! IT WILL LEAD TO A DISASTROUS EF-
FECT; ONE THAT MAY VERY WELL OCCUR OVER
AND OVER AGAIN.

I HAVE SAID BEFORE, WORKING WITH DEMONS
IS A "QUID PRO QUO" ARRANGEMENT. YOU MUST
FIND SOMETHING THE DEMON WANTS IN RETURN
FOR WHAT YOU ARE ASKING. IT IS NOT A NEGOTIA-
TION HOWEVER, YOU MUST GIVE, JUST AS YOU
WOULD MAKE AN OFFERING TO SATAN HIMSELF
IN EXCHANGE FOR YOUR DESIRE. THIS IS NOT THE
FOLK LORE OF SELLING ONE'S SOUL TO SATAN. THAT
IDEA WAS CREATED BY THE XTIAN CHURCH TO

FRIGHTEN ANYONE WHO WOULD BE SO BOLD AS TO INTERACT IN THE MAGICAL MEDIUM. SATAN DOES NOT WANT YOUR SOUL!

ALL HUMANS ARE BORN WITH THE ABILITY TO NAVIGATE THE ASTRAL PLANE HOWEVER, THROUGH SYSTEMATICALLY "CHIPPING AWAY OF THE CRE-ATIVE SIDE" OF A CHILD (METAPHORICALLY SPEAK-ING), THIS BRIDGE IS SLOWLY DESTROYED FOREVER. A CHILD 5 YEARS OLD WILL CERTAINLY HAVE A DIF-FERENT OUTLOOK OF THEIR REALITY THAN A CHILD OF 15 YEARS OLD. WE MUST UNDERSTAND EACH ONE OF US IS AN <u>INDIVIDUAL</u> AND IF YOU ARE READING THIS BOOK, YOU WERE ONCE A CHILD AND YOU PROBABLY WILL REMEMBER THE TIME WHEN YOU COULD DO THINGS MAGICALLY; WHETHER IT WAS WISHING FOR SOMETHING TO COME TRUE OR WISHING A TEACHER WOULD (OR WOULD NOT) CALL UPON YOU IN CLASS. YOU MAY BE ABLE TO REMEMBER A TIME WHEN YOU COULD MANIPULATE MAGIC.

AS WE GROW OLDER, THE WORLD BEATS THE DE-SIRE OUT OF US; WEARING US DOWN INTO CON-FORMITY AND SUBMISSION HOWEVER, WE ALWAYS RETAIN THE MAGICAL ABILITY. WE FORGET THE

SUBTLE NUANCES AND METHODS AS WE BECOME RELEGATED TO NOTHING MORE THAN WHAT THE WORLD DESIRES OF US. THOSE WHO THINK FOR THEMSELVES HAVE BEEN, AND ALWAYS WILL BE, A THREAT TO ESTABLISHED RELIGIONS. RELIGION MUST RELY UPON "SELLING THEIR LIE" OVER AND OVER AGAIN. PEOPLE, THROUGH REPEATED BRAINWASHING OVER TIME, ACCEPT THE LIE.

WHAT IS YOUR EARLIEST MEMORY WHEN YOU WERE A CHILD? DO YOU REMEMBER SOMETHING HAPPENING TO YOU; DO YOU REMEMBER YOUR FIRST OR SECOND BIRTHDAY? MANY CHILDREN BEGIN TO REALLY REMEMBER (RECOLLECTION) WHEN BECOMING CONSCIOUS AROUND THE AGE OF 2 TO 4 YEARS OLD. THE CONSCIOUSNESS OF A CHILD DEVELOPS THE CHILD'S MEMORY JUST AS EXPLAINED IN THE LAW OF INTENSITY; THE MORE VIVID THE EXPERIENCE, THE MORE A PERSON REMEMBERS IT. THE LAW OF INTENSITY ALSO HELPS A PERSON TO LEARN; IF THEY HAVE A VIVID LEARNING EXPERIENCE, THOSE THINGS LEAVE A MARK ON A PERSONS PSYCHE.

IF SOMEONE WERE TO STICK A GUN IN YOUR FACE AND TELL YOU THAT THEY WERE GOING TO

KILL YOU, I FIRMLY BELIEVE YOU WOULD RE-
MEMBER THAT EVENT FOR THE REST OF YOUR LIFE.
THAT WILL ALWAYS BE A CONSTANT REMINDER OF
HOW 'EVIL' THE WORLD CAN TRULY BE.

OUR EXPERIENCES REINFORCE OUR BELIEFS; IF
WE BELIEVE THE WORLD IS A HAPPY PLACE AND
OUR EXPERIENCES AGREE WITH THAT BELIEF, WE
WILL PERCEIVE OUR REALITY AS BEING A "WARM
AND LOVING PLACE". IF YOU HAVE BEEN ABUSED
BY YOUR FAMILY MEMBERS AT AN EARLY AGE
AND HAD TO PROSTITUTE YOURSELF IN ORDER TO
SURVIVE, YOU PROBABLY HAVE A LOW EXPECTA-
TION OF YOUR FELLOW HUMAN BECAUSE THOSE
EVENTS WERE SO VIVID, YOU WILL NEVER FORGET
THOSE THINGS. YOUR BELIEF SYSTEM IS BASED
UPON THOSE EVENTS.

THE WAY PEOPLE HAVE TREATED YOU, UP UN-
TIL THIS POINT WHERE YOU ARE READING THESE
WORDS, HAS MOLDED HOW YOU PERCEIVE YOUR
REALITY. IF HOWEVER, THE WAY YOU HAVE BEEN
TREATED AND THE WAY THE WORLD IS PERCEIVED BY
YOU DIFFERS GREATLY FROM YOUR BELIEFS, PER-
HAPS YOU BECOME A PESSIMIST AND HAVE A NEG-
ATIVE VIEW OF LIFE. PERHAPS YOU DO NOT BELIEVE

BECAUSE YOU HAVE HEARD SO MANY LIES IN THE PAST. PERHAPS YOU ARE SIMPLY AFRAID TO BELIEVE, WHICH IS, IN SOME CIRCUMSTANCES, PERFECTLY 'NATURAL'. SOME HAVE ALLOWED INDIVIDUALS INTO THEIR LIFE, INTO THEIR COMFORT AREA ONLY TO BE BRUISED AND BEATEN (METAPHORICALLY SPEAKING).

THE WAY YOU ARE PERCEIVING THESE WORDS IS BASED UPON YOUR PAST AND THE WAY YOU HAVE EXPERIENCED THE WORLD; THE WAY THE WORLD HAS TREATED YOU. MAYBE YOU HAVE MADE SOME BAD CHOICES AND NOW YOUR LIFE HAS BROUGHT YOU TO WHERE YOU ARE NOW; THROUGH NO ONE'S FAULT BUT YOUR OWN. I KNOW NO ONE WANTS TO ACCEPT THAT TRUTH HOWEVER, DO NOT LIE TO YOURSELF.

WHAT I PERCEIVE MAY NOT BE WHAT YOU PERCEIVE. OUR REALITIES MAY BE TOTALLY DIFFERENT EVEN THOUGH WE STAND TOGETHER IN THE SAME PLACE. REALITY AND SPATIAL AWARENESS IS QUITE DIFFERENT THAN THE REALITY OF A SITUATION. PEOPLE OFTEN CONFUSE THE TWO CONCEPTS BUT THEY ARE REALLY EASY TO UNDERSTAND. YOU PERCEIVE WITH YOUR SENSES; YOU SEE WITH YOUR

EYES AND HEAR WITH YOUR EARS AND IF YOU WERE TO TAKE ONE MOMENT OUT OF TIME AND ANALYZE IT, YOU MIGHT SEE THAT YOUR PERCEPTION WAS NOT THE SAME AS THE WORLD'S PERCEPTION. PERHAPS YOU COULD SEE MORE THAN OTHERS COULD SEE. IT BECOMES PAINFULLY OBVIOUS AT TIMES THAT THOSE WHO ARE WILLING TO LEARN, SEEKING KNOWLEDGE, WILL FIND KNOWLEDGE.

AS A PERSON BECOMES BUSIER AND BUSIER, HE / SHE TENDS TO OVERLOOK THE SIMPLEST OF THINGS. YOU HAVE HEARD THE SAYING "THE PERSON CANNOT SEE THE FOREST FOR THE TREES". THIS IS VERY ACCURATE AT TIMES. SUCH AN ANTIDOTE IS GLARINGLY OBVIOUS. SOME INDIVIDUALS SIMPLY REFUSED TO SEE WHAT IS IN FRONT OF THEM. IF YOU WERE TO ASK AN INDIVIDUAL WHAT THEY 'WANT TO SEE' AS OPPOSED TO 'WHAT THEY TRULY SEE', YOU WILL FIND SOME COMMON DENOMINATORS.

THERE ARE CERTAIN THINGS IN THE PARALLAX DIMENSION THAT ARE JUST UNEXPLAINABLE....THEN AGAIN, THERE ARE THOSE THINGS THAT ARE EXPLAINABLE HOWEVER, YOU MUST HAVE THE KNOWLEDGE TO FULLY COMPREHEND. EXPLAINING IT WOULD BE NO DIFFERENT

THAN A CHEMIST WHO SENT YOU AN EQUATION FOR YOU TO CREATE AN INERT GAS. IF YOU HAVE THE KNOWLEDGE TO APPLY THE EQUATION, YOU CAN CERTAINLY PRODUCE THE RESULT BUT IF YOU DO NOT HAVE A FIRM GRASP ON CHEMISTRY, NO ILLUSTRATION WILL HELP. YOU MUST HAVE A BASIC UNDERSTANDING OF CHEMISTRY TO APPLY THAT WHICH IS OF CHEMISTRY.

IF YOU WANT TO SOLVE A MATHEMATICAL EQUATION BUT DO NOT HAVE AN UNDERSTANDING OF MATHEMATICS, NO AMOUNT OF ILLUSTRATION IS GOING TO HELP SOLVE THE EQUATION.

MAGIC IS THE SAME WAY. WITHOUT A FULL GRASP OF MAGIC AND THE ELEMENTS THAT CREATE MAGIC, THERE WILL ALWAYS BE DISTANCE BETWEEN THE MAGICAL OPERATION DESIRED AND THE PRACTITIONER; IT IS THAT SIMPLE. YOU CANNOT CREATE THAT WHICH YOU DO NOT UNDERSTAND! YOU SHOULD NOT DISMISS THAT WHICH YOU CANNOT FULLY GRASP; YOU MUST LEARN THE ART AND SCIENCE OF MAGIC TO FULLY BENEFIT FROM THE FULL POTENTIAL.

MAGIC HAS LIMITATIONS BUT KNOWING HOW MAGIC WORKS AND APPLYING THOSE SIMPLE

TECHNIQUES CREATES THE BUILDING BLOCKS OF MAGICAL OPERATIONS. WHETHER YOU BELIEVE YOU CAN LEARN FROM INVESTING 20 MINUTES READING A BOOK OR WHETHER YOU MUST INVEST COUNTLESS HOURS AND YEARS AND UNTOLD EX-PENSE TO ACQUIRE THE NECESSARY SKILLS TO BE-COME PROFICIENT, IT WILL TAKE TIME AND EFFORT ON YOUR PART. THERE ARE NO SHORTCUTS WHEN LEARNING THAT WHICH YOU WHOLEHEARTEDLY DE-SIRE. THERE ARE NO SHORTCUTS!!

MAGIC IS A HIGHLY EVOLVED, HIGHLY ME-CHANICAL, THEORETICAL ART AND MAGIC CON-SUMES NOT ONLY KNOWLEDGE, ENERGY AND SKILL, IT ~~WILL~~ "MUST" TOTALLY CONSUME THE PRACTITIONER!

IT'S NOT THE FALL THAT KILLS YOU; IT'S THE SUDDEN STOP. WHEN YOU FINALLY REALIZE THAT YOUR LIFE MAY HAVE BEEN IN VAIN, THAT IS THE DAY OF RECKONING. FOR MANY PEOPLE WHO HAVE BEEN SUBJECTED TO MENTAL, PHYSICAL AND SPIRITUAL TORTURE AND ABUSE, THAT DAY OF RECKONING CAN TAKE ONE OF SEVERAL DIFFERENT FORMS. FOR EXAMPLE, WHEN A PERSON WHO HAS BEEN PHYSICALLY ABUSED FINALLY REACHES THE

POINT WHERE THEY SAY "NO MORE", THEY CAN TURN VIOLENT AND FOCUS THE PAIN TOWARD THOSE WHO HAVE INFLICTED SUCH INJURY UP ON THEM FOR SO LONG. THEY ARE NO LONGER "THE VICTIM"; FAR FROM IT!

FOR THOSE WHO HAVE SUFFERED AT THE HANDS OF SO-CALLED SPIRITUAL LEADERS, THE DAY OF RECKONING MAY TAKE A DIFFERENT FORM. HE / SHE MAY THROW OFF THE CHAINS OF BONDAGE AND SEE THE SITUATION FOR WHAT IT TRULY IS; A MAN-MADE INSTITUTION DESIGNED TO CONTROL OTHER PEOPLE.

THROWING THE CHAINS FROM ONE'S SHOULDERS AND FORGING A NEW LIFE BASED UPON DESIRE AS OPPOSED TO DOGMA IS A TRUE REALIZATION AND A TRUE SPIRITUAL AWAKENING THAT EVERYONE DE-SERVES TO EXPERIENCE IN THEIR LIFETIME. WHILE THERE ARE THOSE WHO MAKE THEIR WAY THROUGH LIFE AS SLAVES, OTHERS WANT TO BELIEVE IN SOMETHING SPIRITUAL. FOR THESE PEOPLE, THERE ARE PLENTY OF SHYSTERS AND LIARS TO FILL THE VOID.

PART II - CLAVIS AUREA

Vom Licht in die Dunkelheit auf dem Pfad des Kleinsten Wiederstandes reist unsere Kraft. Es ist wichtig für die Hexe dieses Konzept zu verstehen.

DE PROFUNDUS

I WOULD LIKE TO SHARE MY CLOSEST DEMONIC RELATIONSHIPS WHICH I HAVE BUILT OVER TWO DECADES. THESE DEMONS ARE WILLING TO FORGE ALLIANCES WITH SATANISTS (AND OTHER PRACTITIONERS) AND I HAVE EXPERIENCED GREAT SUCCESS (ALONE AND WITH MAGNUM OPUS) THANKS TO THESE SATANIC DEMONS.

HERE IS MY WORD OF CAUTION: AS I HAVE STATED NUMEROUS TIMES, YOU MUST TREAT DEMONS WITH UTMOST RESPECT. THOSE INDIVIDUALS WHO DESIRE A DEMON'S ASSISTANCE MUST BE WILLING (AND ABLE) TO PROVIDE AN OFFERING OF COMPARABLE MEASURE. DEMONS ARE STRONG SATANIC ALLIES HOWEVER, IF YOU ACT WITH IMPUNITY, YOU WILL EXPERIENCE WRATH AS YOU HAVE NEVER IMAGINED.

I HAVE SUGGESTED SATANIC STONES, THE COLOR OF CANDLES, INCENSE AND OTHER INFORMATION I BELIEVE VALUABLE. I AM ONLY SHARING WHAT HAS PRODUCED SUCCESS FOR ME AND OUR COVEN IN THE PAST. AS WITH ANYTHING, DO NOT BE AFRAID TO ATTEMPT VARIATIONS OF THE APPLICA-

TIONS. IF THE CHANGES ARE NOT EFFECTIVE.........<u>"NOTHING HAPPENS"</u>.

DEMONS ARE INDIVIDUALS AND AS SUCH, THEY MAY BE ATTRACTED, INTERESTED, UNINTERESTED, MOODY, AND MAY EVEN BECOME VIOLENT IF PROVOKED. KNOW YOUR LIMITATIONS AND RESPECT THE BOUNDARIES, NEVER FORGETTING WHAT YOU HAVE LEARNED IN "SANCTUM OF SHADOWS VOLUME I" AND IN PART I OF THIS BOOK.

IF YOU DESIRE TO CALL UPON AN UNFAMILIAR DEMON, I STRONGLY RECOMMEND ASKING SATAN TO ATTEND THE RITUAL AS YOUR ADVOCATE (INTERMEDIARY). OVER TIME, PERHAPS YOU WILL BUILD A STRONG BOND WITH THESE "FRIENDS FROM JUST BEYOND THE REALM"!

THE DESCRIPTIONS OF THESE DEMONS ARE FROM MY PERSPECTIVE AND HOW I HAVE EXPERIENCED AND INTERACTED WITH THEM. YOU MAY DISAGREE WITH MY ASSESSMENTS HOWEVER, PLEASE DO NOT SOPHOMORICALLY CLAIM I AM WRONG JUST BECAUSE IT DOES NOT ALIGN WITH YOUR BELIEFS.

READY? SATANIC BLESSINGS......ENJOY!

PRINCE BALAN

SYMBOLUM

BALAN

BALAN IS A PRINCE OF HELL; A SATANIC DE-
MON OF TRUTH, GREAT POWER, AND SATANIC
STRATEGY. HE EASILY FORETELLS THE FUTURES OF
HIS BELOVED FOLLOWERS AND FOR THIS REASON, HE
CAN PROVIDE VALUABLE ADVICE; AN EXPERT OF
COUNTERMEASURES; THE DEFENSE TO COUNTER THE
MAGIC OF THE PRACTITIONER'S ADVERSARIES
(KNOWN OR UNKNOWN). HE REIGNS OVER A
VAST UNION OF "PROTECTORS" (40 LEGIONS
STRONG); HOLDING FOREVER SACRED THE SECRETS OF
THE KINGDOM OF LORD BELIAL.

BALAN IS A GREAT TEACHER OF TACTICAL

METHODOLOGIES ENABLING THE PRACTITIONER TO DEFEND AGAINST RAVENOUS OPPONENTS (SPELLS/ CURSES[15]) WHILE FOCUSING THE BRUNT OF A COUNTERATTACK DEEP INTO THE OPPONENT'S CHEST.

HE IS A MASTER OF ILLUSION AND THE USE OF NATURAL CAMOUFLAGE; OFTEN FADING INTO A VISTA (LANDSCAPE, SEASCAPE, ETC.) BEFORE THE OP- PONENT REALIZES BALAN'S ABSENCE. THE PRACTI- TIONER SHOULD CONSIDER USING BLUE TOPAZ WHILE BURNING VANILLA INCENSE. RED CANDLES WORK WELL AS EVIDENCED BY PAST SUCCESSES I HAVE EXPERIENCED.

BALAN WILL OFTEN BE THE FIRST TO PHYSICAL- LY MANIFEST DURING THE PRACTITIONER'S RITUAL. HE MAY "CLEAR THE SANCTUM OR RITUAL ROOM" OF NEGATIVE ENERGY BEFORE OTHERS APPEAR.

HE MAY SILENTLY OBSERVE A FEW MOMENTS OF A RITUAL BEFORE REVEALING HIMSELF TO THE COVEN MEMBERS. A MASTER OF "BLENDING INTO SURROUNDINGS" ALLOWS BALAN TO REMAIN HID- DEN; ALTHOUGH FULLY TRANSVERSED THROUGH THE 'DOORWAY' OF THE PARALLAX DIMENSION.

---

[15] See the "Macbeth Curse"

A COMMON CHARACTERISTIC OF BALAN'S MANIFESTATION IS HIS CHOSEN POINT OF ENTRY INTO THE INNER SANCTUM; FROM THE NORTHEAST AND MAY BE ACCOMPANIED BY THE DEMON BARUCHAS.

I HAVE FOUND CONSISTENT SUCCESS WHEN CALLING UPON BALAN AND ABRAXAS (AKA RULER OF THE 365 HEAVENS) SIMULTANEOUSLY. THESE TWO ARE VERY COMPATIBLE TOGETHER AND CONTRIBUTE TO A MARKED INCREASE IN SATANIC ENERGY. THE PRACTITIONER SHOULD REWARD BOTH GREATLY, SIGNIFYING HIS / HER GRATITUDE. AS A RESULT, THEY WILL INDEED SMILE UPON YOUR FUTURE WORKS!

OF ALL SATANIC DEMONS, BALAN PROVES TO BE THE MOST BENEFICIAL DURING WORKINGS THAT REQUIRE A GLIMPSE INTO THE FUTURE (OUR LIMITED REALM OF TIME). HE OFTEN PROVIDES A CLEAR VISION OF THE FUTURE STATE, INCLUDING THE PATH ONE MUST TRAVEL IN ORDER TO AVOID UNDESIRABLE OUTCOMES OCCURRING AS A RESULT OF THE SPECIFIC MAGICAL OPERATION BEING CONDUCTED. THE BEST TIME TO CALL UPON BALAN IS EARLY MORNING, JUST BEFORE DAWN.

PRINCE BALAN IS A PROFICIENT ASTRAL GUIDE AND COUPLED WITH HIS TRUTHFUL (AND ACCURATE) EVALUATION AND GUIDANCE, HE ALLOWS THE PRACTITIONER TO CIRCUMVENT THE ASTRAL PLANES "BETTER LEFT UNTRAVELLED" AND HAS <u>MORE THAN ONCE</u>, PROVIDED COUNCIL, PREVENTING ME FROM STEPPING INTO THE WELL-LAID SNARE OF AN ADVERSARY DESIRING TO HARM ME IN SOME MANNER.

LOYALTY TO BALAN IS A KEY (REQUIRED) ATTRIBUTE FOR HIS FOLLOWERS. HE MAY ANSWER THE CALL OF AN ADVERSARY WISHING HARM FOR ONE OF BALAN'S LOYAL DEVOTEES. BY DOING SO, BALAN EASILY LEARNS OF THE ADVERSARY'S STRATEGY, WHILE "LULLING" THE ADVERSARY INTO A FALSE SENSE OF 'CONTROL'.

ALWAYS THE PROFICIENT TACTICIAN, BALAN GUIDES THE ADVERSARY TO HIS / HER OWN DEMISE; USUALLY HARVESTING RETURNING DEEDS, CULMINATING WITH A "STRATEGIC PLACEMENT" OF THE ADVERSARY'S OWN ATHAME!

"ACHTUNG! ALLES FÜR SIE,
WENN IM HERZEN BRENNT DAS FEUER
FREUT SICH DAS SCHWARZE UNGEHEUER"

Ordnung ist der Stamm einer gut geführten Gruppe. Caos züchtet Caos und Zerrüttung des Zirkels.

EARL RÄUM

SYMBOLUM
RÄUM

RÄUM IS AN EARL OF HELL WHO IS THE FRIENDLIEST AND MOST ACCOMMODATING OF ALL SATANIC DEMONS I HAVE EVER EXPERIENCED; MOST SURPRISING SINCE HE COMMANDS A FORCE OF 30 LEGIONS. ALONG WITH HIS BROTHERS PRINCE MALPHAS (30 LEGIONS), MARQUIS ANDRAS (30 LEGIONS) AND MARQUIS MARCHOSIAS (30 LEGIONS), RÄUM'S SPAN OF DEMONIC INFLUENCE IS FAR-REACHING AND EFFECTIVE. VERY FEW INCANTATIONS EVADE HIS ATTENTION.

I WAS NOT AWARE OF RÄUM UNTIL READING "SILENTIUM IN PERSONA DIABOLI" WHICH I RE-

CEIVED FROM MY PATRIARCHAL COVEN WHILE IN BAVARIA, GERMANY. RÄUM IS REFERENCED 13 TIMES (NOT BY COINCIDENCE) THROUGHOUT THE SATANIC GRIMOIRE.

I RECOMMEND NEW PRACTITIONERS CALL UPON RÄUM DURING THEIR FIRST MANIFESTATION RITUAL. I HAVE RECEIVED 100% POSITIVE FEEDBACK FROM THOSE ACOLYTES FOLLOWING MY RECOMMENDATION. HE IS JOVIAL AND ALWAYS SHOWS APPRECIATION FOR SPECIAL CONSIDERATIONS OF THE PRACTITIONER.

SUNSTONE APPEALS GREATLY TO RÄUM'S CHARACTER, ALTHOUGH PRECIOUS STONES SUCH AS BLUE SAPPHIRES ARE MOST FREQUENTLY USED. USE ROYAL BLUE CANDLES AROUND YOUR ALTAR AND BERGAMOT EXTRACT OR CORIANDER (HEATED OVER THE FLAME) CREATES A PLEASING AROMATIC ATMOSPHERE.

THE BEST TIME OF YEAR TO CALL UPON RÄUM IS WALSPURGISNACHT. CALL UPON HIM IN THE VERY EARLY MORNING, JUST AFTER THE MIDNIGHT (WITCHING) HOUR. HE WILL ALSO APPEAR FOR A SATANIC WEDDING IF CALLED BY THE ATTENDING MAGUS. THE BRIDE IS EXPECTED TO RECIPROCATE

THE "GOOD DEED"........INDEED!

FOR THE PRACTITIONER WISHING TO STEAL, VIEW, EXTRACT OR "PLANT" DISINFORMATION USING MAGIC AGAINST HIS / HER ENEMIES, RÄUM PROVES CONSISTENTLY PROFICIENT. HE WILL OFTEN APPEAR IN THE MIDST OF A FIRST-TIME DABBLER, LEARN HIS / HER LIMITATIONS, PERFORM IMPROMPTU RECONNAISSANCE AND DISAPPEAR.

JUST LIKE A TROJAN WARRIOR, RÄUM WILL RE-VEAL THE INFORMATION TO HIS LOYAL FOLLOWER(S) OR EXPLOIT THE KNOWLEDGE LATER FOR PERSONAL GAINS.....THE ENEMY WILL REMAIN NONE-THE-WISER.

RÄUM WILL PROVIDE ANSWERS FOR THE PRAC-TITIONER HOWEVER, HE EXPECTS TO BE COMPENSAT-ED. HE MAY APPEAR IN ANY RITUAL OR CEREMO-NY INVOLVING A YOUNG GIRL AND HE IS QUITE FOND OF THOSE WHO ARE SMALL IN STATURE.

AS WITH A NUMBER OF DEMONS, RÄUM HAS A VORACIOUS SEXUAL APPETITE. HIS ECLECTIC TASTES FOR "ALL THINGS SEXUAL" IS MATCHED ONLY BY HIS STAMINA AND ABILITY TO ITERATIVELY PER-FORM TIME-AFTER-TIME-AFTER-TIME. HAVING AN ALTAR THAT FITS HIS PREFERENCES IS MOST ADVAN-

TAGEOUS FOR THE PRACTITIONER.

PRINCE CAYM

SYMBOLUM

CAYM

CAYM (AKA CAMIO) COMMANDS AN INFER-
NAL DEMONIC FORCE OF 30 LEGIONS. HE IS HIGH-
LY INTELLIGENT; A SKILLFUL ORATOR, LOGICIAN
AND CRITICAL THINKER...."PAR EXCELLENCE".

HE ROUTINELY DEMONSTRATES HIS "LIGHT-
NING-FAST" COGNITIVE ABILITY TO PERFORM DE-
DUCTIVE REASONING; QUICKLY WEEDING-OUT
AND REPLACING RHETORIC WITH PASSIONATE PER-
SUASION WHILE REMOVING DISSENTING OPINIONS,
SKILLFULLY REPLACING THOSE DISSENTS WITH VI-
ABLE ALTERNATIVES OF HIS OWN!

CAYM IS TRUTHFUL IN HIS ABILITY TO FORE-

TELL THE FUTURE; WHETHER FAVORABLE OR UNFA-
VORABLE, CAYM REFUSES TO PUT A POSITIVE SPIN
ON OMINOUS REVELATIONS. MY ADVICE REGARD-
ING HIS BEDSIDE MANNER: "IF YOU DO NOT WANT
TO KNOW, DO NOT ASK THE QUESTION!"

AQUA BLUE APATITE APPEALS GREATLY TO
CAYM. USE ROYAL BLUE CANDLES AROUND YOUR
ALTAR AND BURN LOTUS INCENSE. THE BEST TIME
OF YEAR TO CALL UPON CAYM IS ALL HALLOWS
EVE. CALL UPON HIM IN THE EARLY EVENING,
JUST AFTER DUSK.

CAYM HAS THE REMARKABLE ABILITY TO CON-
VERSE WITH ALL MEMBERS OF THE EARTHLY ANI-
MAL KINGDOM. HIS ADVICE AS TO YOUR SELEC-
TION OF DEMONIC FAMILIAR IS INVALUABLE.

AS WITH MOST HIGHLY INTELLIGENT INDIVID-
UALS, CAYM WILL QUICKLY GROW IMPATIENT
WITH A HUMAN'S LACK OF UNDERSTANDING,
POINTLESS QUESTIONS, IGNORANCE AND / OR CON-
DESCENSION; WHETHER INTENTIONAL OR NOT.

YOU DO NOT WANT TO TEST CAYM'S RE-
SOLVE.....THIS IS NOT THE SATANIC DEMON TO
PLAY AROUND WITH FOR HE WILL REVEAL HIS
SWORD AND FLAY YOU, HEAD TO TOE!

FRAU PERCHTA

SYMBOLUM

FRAU PERCHTA

FRAU PERCHTA (AKA FRAU BERCHTA) IS A SOR-CERESS WHOSE INSPIRATION HAS CONTRIBUTED GREATLY TO THE GRIMOIRE "SILENTIUM IN PER-SONA DIABOLI" WHICH WAS ITERATIVELY WRITTEN IN THE LATE 1400s. I RECEIVED A COPY OF THE GRIMOIRE IN DECEMBER 2012 WHILE IN BAVARIA.

THE GRIMOIRE WAS ASSEMBLED FROM 'LITERAL LIFETIMES' OF PASSING THE INFORMATION THROUGH THE LINEAGE AND PERSISTENT PRACTICE. THE OUTPUT OF SUCH DEDICATION AND DEVOTION IS A GRIMOIRE OF KNOWLEDGE, DOCUMENTATION

AND METICULOUS TRANSCRIPTION. I HAVE SHARED
PERTINENT SECTIONS IN <u>SANCTUM OF SHADOWS
VOLUME I: THE SATANIST</u>.

FRAU PERCHTA (REFERRED TO AS AN ALPEN
DÄMONEN) IS ASSOCIATED WITH MANY ALUMNI
SPIRITS ORIGINATING IN SWABIA AND BAVARIA,
INCLUDING FRAU HOLDA; A PROTECTORESS FOUND
IN RHINE, MÜNSTEREIFEL AND BEETGUM IN-
SCRIPTIONS WRITTEN IN LATIN; CIRCA 200 ANNO
DOMINIK.

GREATLY ASSOCIATED WITH GERMAN FOLKLORE
AND HISTORY, THE FRAU HAS JOINED THE RANKS
OF "HEXEN ASKESIS ALPEN DÄMONEN"; THOSE BE-
INGS KNOWN AS ALPS; DEMONIC, SEXUALLY-
CHARGED ELVES OR IMPS.

FRAU PERCHTA HAS CONTRIBUTED TO MY WRIT-
INGS ON DEMONIC RITUALS FOUND IN VARIOUS
BLOG POSTS ON MY <u>SATANIC MAGIC</u> BLOG. SHE AP-
PEARS IN PHYSICAL FORM AND FACILITATES MY
WRITING PROCESS; CREATING VARIATIONS ON ES-
TABLISHED WORKINGS AS SHE SERVES AS MUSE AND
SUCCUBUS; STIMULATING MY SATANIC THOUGHTS
AND REVIVING PRACTICES OF LONG AGO.

THE FRAU ACTS AS PATRIARCH OF 5 LEGIONS OF

ALPS, PERPETUATING A CONTINUUM OF DEMONS OFTEN MISUNDERSTOOD BY PRACTITIONERS WHO ARE UNABLE OR UNWILLING TO LEARN THEIR SUBTLE NUANCES; WHICH GREATLY HINDERS ADVANCEMENT INTO HIGHER PROCESSES.

AS THE SORCERESS OF ALPS, FRAU PERCHTA INFLUENCES DREAMS AND CAN DIRECT THE VISIONS OF A PRACTITIONER BY ELEVATING THE EFFECTIVE ATTRIBUTES WITHIN THE SUBCONSCIOUS; SIMULTANEOUSLY OPENING A 'TRANSCENDENTAL DOORWAY' TO THE ASTRAL PLANE. THIS PORTAL ALLOWS COGNITIVE TRANSITIONING OF THE SATANIC POWERS OF THE MIND WHILE OFFERING GUIDANCE FOR THE PRACTITIONER ALONG THE LHP. THIS GUIDANCE METHODOLOGY IS AS OLD AS RECORDED HISTORY ITSELF HOWEVER, IT REMAINS THE ONLY VIABLE METHOD TO PREVENT LOOSING ONE'S WAY ALONG THE PATH.

THE FRAU IS OFTEN REGARDED AS A GENTLE, HELPFUL AND BENIGN BEING HOWEVER, THROUGH VOLUPTUARY SERVITUDE TO DER TEUFEL (SATAN), SHE IS A SATANIC DEMON WHO IS VERY POWERFUL AND SHOULD NEVER BE CROSSED BY THE PRACTITIONER. HER MEMORY IS ENDLESS AND SHE WILL

TORMENT THOSE WHO TREAT HER WITH IMPUNITY.

ALPS (AKA MARE) ARE MALE INCUBI WHO, BY MAGICAL VIRTUE, VISIT THE OBJECT OF THE MAGICAL OPERATION; SITTING UPON THE CHEST OF THE DOOMED INDIVIDUAL, THUS CAUSING BEWILDERING FEELINGS OF SUFFOCATION AND THE INABILITY TO BREATH.

THIS PHENOMENA, USUALLY OCCURRING BEFORE OR DURING REM SLEEP, INDUCES SLEEP DEPRECATION, RESULTING IN PSYCHOLOGICAL DELIRIUM AND A CEASELESS EROSION OF REALITY. IF A PRACTITIONER IF TARGETED, HIS / HER MAGICAL ABILITIES WILL CONTINUE A DEVOLUTION UNTIL NO LONGER ABLE TO DEFEND AGAINST INCOMING MAGICAL OFFENSES / ATTACKS UTILIZING DEMONIC ENERGY.

FROM THE AREA SURROUNDING VAL CANALE, FRIULI REGION, FRAU PERCHTA IS REFERENCED AS WITNESS AND GUIDE TO THE "GOOD WALKERS" IN RECORDED HISTORY. THE AREA OF FRIULI CAUGHT THE ATTENTION OF THE CATHOLIC CHURCH IN THE LATE SIXTEENTH CENTURY.

FRAU PERCHTA IS ALSO ASSOCIATED WITH THE "WILDE JAGD". HER INSPIRATION IS ALSO SAID TO

HAVE GREATLY CONTRIBUTED TO MANY PRACTI-
TIONERS OF ANTIQUITY SUCH AS POPE JOHN XXI,
WHO WAS ACTUALLY A PRACTICING MAGICIAN
AND IS RUMORED TO HAVE WRITTEN THE "THE-
SAURUS PAUPERUM" UNDER THE ASSUMED ALIAS
"PEDRO HISPANO". THIS ANTHOLOGY IS BETTER
SAVED FOR ONE OF MY FUTURE BOOKS, BECAUSE
THE HISTORY IS QUITE INTERESTING INDEED.

FRAU PERCHTA ENJOYS ANY INCENSE THAT HAS
A CLEAN, FRESH CONNOTATION, REPRESENTATIVE
OF SPRING; THE HOPE AND JOY THE FIRST WARM
DAYS BRING AS THE YEARLY SNOW MELTS AND THE
TENDER FOLIAGE BECOMES ALIVE AGAIN, SPROUT-
ING FROM THE FERTILE EARTH. HER DESIRED STONE
IS AMETHYST.

WALSPURGISNACHT IS THE BEST SUITED NIGHT
TO CALL UPON THE FRAU; "UM HALB EINS NACHT"
(12:30 AM), IF CALLED, SHE WILL APPEAR AND
YOUR REQUEST SHOULD BE ON THE TIP OF YOUR
TONGUE. BLUE AND RED CANDLES SHOULD BE USED
BY THE PRACTITIONER.

AS SHE SENDS HER LEGIONS OF ALPS TO DO YOUR
BIDDING, YOUR RITUAL SHOULD CULMINATE WITH
A FERTILITY RITE IN HER HONOR. MATING AND

THE FERTILITY RITE REPRESENTS THE CONTINUOUS-
NESS OF LIFE; THE PRECIOUS ACT THAT ENSURES THE
VERY SURVIVAL OF THE HUMAN SPECIES.

DUKE ZEPAR

SYMBOLUM

ZEPAR

ZEPAR IS THE COMMANDER OF 26 LEGIONS OF DEMONS. HE IS A FIERCE WARRIOR AND IS ABLE TO BRING ABOUT CRUSHING BLOWS TO YOUR OPPONENTS. HE IS BRAZEN AND BOLD; AFTER HE HAS ATTACKED, THE MATTER IS QUICKLY DECIDED. HIS TECHNIQUE IS ONLY SECOND TO ONE; SAMAEL, THE "DEMON OF DEATH".

SOME WRITERS HAVE ASSERTED ZEPAR USES PEDERASTY TO ATTRACT MEN (AND OTHER DEMONS) TO HIS COMMAND HOWEVER, THAT CLAIM IS WITH OUR MERIT AND TOTALLY FALSE.

RED IS DUKE ZEPAR'S COLOR AND THE INNER

SANCTUM IS ROUTINELY PREPARED IN A 'GOTHIC' RED AMBIENCE BEFORE CALLING UPON HIM FOR ASSISTANCE. HE IS VERY SEXUALLY PROVOCATIVE AND BELIEVES (AS I BELIEVE) IN A LIBERAL DOSE OF ORAL PLEASURING; USING THE TONGUE ON THE VULVA, CLITORIS AND GRÄFENBERG SPOT.

AS THE MOST VOCAL OF ALL DEMONS, ZEPAR OFTEN SCREAMS, YELLS, AND SNARLS. WHEN HE DISPLAYS HIS FIRE-RED ARMORED BODY, MOST BEINGS WILL QUICKLY SCATTER, WHICH REDUCES THE POSSIBILITY OF ANOTHER DEMON (PERHAPS SENT BY YOUR ENEMY) "CRASHING" YOUR CHAMBER. MUCH AS AN ALPHA MALE ANIMAL, I HAVE WITNESSED HIS IMPOSITION OF POWER UPON OTHERS; WHICH IS QUITE FRIGHTENING.

MANY FROM BEYOND THE PARALLAX DIMENSION ARE MISUNDERSTOOD BECAUSE OF PAST "INDISCRETIONS" WHICH ARE NOT REALLY MISGIVINGS AT ALL. THE MERCY SHOWN TO NEWBORN INFANTS WHO WERE SEVERELY HANDICAPPED OR CRIPPLED IS VIEWED AS BUTCHERY BY TODAY'S STANDARDS HOWEVER, THE WISDOM OF SO MANY GENERATIONS PAST IS STILL VIEWED AS WISDOM; NO MATTER THE OPINION OF THE WITNESS.

FOR THIS REASON, ZEPAR HAS BEEN MISUNDER-
STOOD AT TIMES. HE IS LOUD AND INTIMIDATING
YET THERE IS NO DEMON BETTER TO STAND GUARD
OVER THE COVEN DURING A RITUAL, ALTHOUGH
HE MAY NOT TAKE AN ACTIVE PART IN THE PRO-
CEEDINGS.

SYMBOLIC 'EXPURGATIONS' FOR THE PRACTI-
TIONER ARE SOON FULFILLED IF ZEPAR IS SUM-
MONED AS A GUARDIAN OF THE "INNER DOOR".
HE DUTIFULLY PERFORMS THE MENIAL, YET NEC-
ESSARY, TASKS SUCH AS 'RESTRAINT' WHICH MAY BE
NEEDED BEFORE A SACRIFICE.

ZEPAR ALSO EXTRICATES ALL APPREHENSIVENESS
FROM THE COVEN; TAKING COMFORT IN THE FACT
ZEPAR IS WITHIN CLOSE PROXIMITY AND IS ABLE TO
NEUTRALIZE ANY UNFORESEEN INTERRUPTIONS
MANIFESTING WITHIN OR OUTSIDE THE INNER
SANCTUM. "INHIBITIONS BE GONE!!!"

BLOODSTONE IS ZEPAR'S STONE. USE RED CAN-
DLES AROUND YOUR ALTAR AND BURN PATCHOULI
OIL. THE BEST TIME OF YEAR TO CALL UPON ZEPAR
IS ALL HALLOWS EVE. CALL UPON HIM IN THE
EARLY EVENING, JUST AFTER DUSK.

Der Kreis möge sich ändern, die Magie
Heißt immer gleich....immer.

FÜTGLE

SYMBOLUM

FÜTGLE

FÜTGLE IS A POWERFUL DEMON WHOSE
COMPETENCE AND ASSISTANCE ARE GREATLY
NEEDED FOR TRANSCENDENTAL COMMUNICATION
AND ASTRAL TRAVELS. HE POSSESSES ADVANCED
KNOWLEDGE OF TECHNIQUES AS A "SHIFTER" WHO
CAN TAKE THE FORM OF ANIMALS OR INHABIT
OTHER HUMANS.

DURING THIS PROCESS, FÜTGLE OFTEN PERPLEXES ENEMIES OF THE PRACTITIONER BY ENTERING HIS / HER BODY AND CONTROLLING THE THOUGHTS AND ACTIONS WHILE THE INHABITED IS RENDERED DEFENSELESS TO SUCH POSSESSION.

FÜTGLE IS REFERENCED IN SEVERAL PASSAGES OF SILENTIUM IN PERSONA DIABOLI (CIRCA 1485); IT IS HERE THAT I BEGAN MY EFFORTS TO LEARN FROM HIM THROUGH DUTIFUL WORK, STUDY AND PERSONAL SACRIFICE. HE HAS MANIFESTED SEVERAL TIMES SINCE I RETURNED FROM GERMANY IN JANUARY 2013 AND I CONTINUE TO LEARN AND APPLY NEWLY GAIN TECHNIQUES ACQUIRED THROUGH HIS GUIDANCE.

UNSUBSTANTIATED REPORTS (CIRCA 1941) CLAIM SEVERAL MANIFESTATIONS OF FÜTGLE AT A NAZI "REICH SS LEADERSHIP SCHOOL" (REICHS-FÜHRERSCHULE SS) LOCATED IN GERMANY'S WEWELSBURG CASTLE. WHILE UNVERIFIABLE, THESE CLAIMS ARE CERTAINLY POSSIBLE AND COMPLETELY PLAUSIBLE SINCE CEREMONIES WERE CONDUCTED AT WEWELSBURG BY SS-LEADER HEINRICH HIMMLER, WHO WAS A AVID STUDENT OF THE OCCULT[16].

---

[16] *"Der Mann, der Hitler die Ideen gab" (The man who gave Hitler the ideas)* - Wilfried Daim; 1957

WHEN CALLING UPON FÜTGLE, IT IS BEST TO BE ALONE, USING A SOLITARY OPERATION. HE IS HIGHLY INTELLIGENT AND WILL SPARE NO TIME FOR THE BEGINNER AND WILL REACT HARSHLY TOWARD "DABBLERS" OR THE NAIVE. HIS EXTENT OF PAIN IS BEST DESCRIBED AS "MENTAL ANGUISH"; A TECHNIQUE OF HUMAN TORTURE WHICH FÜTGLE HAS MASTERED OVER THE AEONS. HIS POINT OF ENTRY IS THROUGH THE MIND SO HE BECOMES PRIVY TO THE PRACTITIONERS DEEPEST, DARKEST SECRETS AT ONCE.

A COMMON METHOD HE OFTEN USES REVEALS THE PRACTITIONER'S MOST PRIVATE (AND PERHAPS EMBARRASSING) DEED(S); EXPOSING THEM TO THE WORLD IN AN INSTANT. CROSS FÜTGLE IF YOU DARE FOR THE RESULTS SHALL BE PAINFUL, AGONIZING AND EVERLASTING. BEWARE!

FÜTGLE SPEAKS THE LANGUAGE OF 'LOGIC' AND RATIONALE IS QUITE HIS FORTE. HE WILL SHED LIGHT ON A PRACTITIONER'S MISUNDERSTOOD CONCEPTS ALLOWING FOR A PATIENT AND STEADFAST RESULT. THE PRACTITIONER IS ABLE TO BUILD RESOLVE AND ADVANCED COGNITION, INCREASING THE CAPACITY FOR STRATEGY AND PLAN EXECU-

TION SEEN THROUGH TO THE BITTER END. IN MY OPINION, FÜTGLE IS THE COGNITIVE "TACTICIAN'S - TACTICIAN".

IN STARK CONTRAST, FÜTGLE IS ALSO A SADISTIC DEMON WHO ENJOYS VERBALLY BELITTLING AND MOCKING A DABBLER'S CRIES WHILE SODOMIZING HIM / HER AS PUNISHMENT FOR 'STUPIDITY AND ARROGANCE'. FÜTGLE REQUIRES SINCERITY FROM THE PRACTITIONER AND HE CAN QUICKLY ASCERTAIN THE INTENT AND MOTIVES OF THE PRACTITIONER. THOSE FOOLS WHO BELIEVE DEMONS ARE 'LAP DOGS' WILLING TO SIT, ROLLOVER AND PLEASE THE "MASTER", THE HARD REALIZATION OF BEING "OUT OF HIS / HER DEPTH" SETS IN "A LITTLE TOO LATE".

DO NOT CONFUSE THIS WITH LUST; THIS IS ABOUT PUNISHMENT, SEVER TORTURE AND CONTROL; THIS IS ABOUT TEACHING THE OFFENDER A LESSON CONCERNING THE PRICE OF IGNORANCE AND EGO.....NOTHING MORE!

IF YOU ARE FACING EAST WHEN CALLING UPON FÜTGLE, HE WILL APPEAR TO YOUR RIGHT; TRANSVERSING THE PARALLAX DIMENSION AND ENTERING OUR REALITY FROM THE SOUTHEAST. HE

IS USUALLY QUIET AND CAUSES VERY LITTLE DIS-
RUPTION IF YOU ARE PRACTICING SATANIC MEDI-
TATION. HE HAS OFTEN MANIFESTED WHILE MY
EYES WERE CLOSED AND I WOULD DISCOVER HIS
PRESENCE WHEN FINISHING MY MEDITATION.

HEMATITE IS FÜTGLE'S STONE. USE BLACK CAN-
DLES AROUND YOUR ALTAR AND BURN SAGE. THE
BEST TIME OF YEAR TO CALL UPON FÜTGLE IS ALL
HALLOWS EVE. CALL UPON HIM IN THE EARLY
MORNING HOURS, JUST AFTER MIDNIGHT.

Dieser Zirkel ist der Grundstein für Magie

Magie ist der Anlass für den Hexenzirkel

ET FACTA EST LUX

I EXPERIENCED THE FIRST DEMONIC MANIFESTA-
TION MANY YEARS AGO. IT SEEMS LIKE A LIFE-
TIME OF WORKING WITH SATANIC AND DEMONIC
BEINGS WOULD HAVE MELLOWED ME TO THE POINT
OF "ROUTINE" HOWEVER, IT HAS ACTUALLY AF-
FECTED ME QUITE THE OPPOSITE. I AM ALWAYS EX-
CITED AND IN AWE WHEN EXPERIENCING A VISIT
FROM THE OTHER REALM.

ALTHOUGH MAGICAL OPERATIONS ARE VERY
MUCH RIGOROUS EVENTS OF STATIC ACTIONS, THE
PASSION CONTINUES TO BURN DEEP WITHIN MY
VERY BEING. EXCITEMENT IS CONTAGIOUS AND
NOTHING PROVES THIS POINT MORE THAN SUCCESS
BEYOND MY DREAMS. I AM NOT ALONE IN THE
JOURNEY AND WHILE THERE ARE LAZY, STUPID
AND NAIVE INDIVIDUALS WHO EXPECT A SHORT-
CUT, THE MAJORITY OF THOSE SEEKING KNOWL-
EDGE RECOGNIZE AND RESPECT THE WORK THEY
MUST DO IN ORDER TO BECOME SUCCESSFUL IN
THEIR OWN RITE.

EVERY INDIVIDUAL MOTIVE BEGINS WITH DE-
SIRE; FROM CONCEPT TO FRUITION, A SEARCHER EN-

TERS THE LEFT HAND PATH TO ENLIGHTENMENT. WHILE THE DESTINATION REMAINS THE ULTIMATE OBJECTIVE, THE TRIP CAN BE LIKEWISE FILLED WITH ACCOMPLISHMENTS, LESSONS AND MICRO-PROCESSES OF LEARNING. ENJOY THE DESTINATION BUT SAVOR THE JOURNEY. THE TASTIEST OF MEALS REQUIRES TIME TO ADEQUATELY PREPARE. SHOULD ANY STEP IN THE PROCESS BE OMITTED OR HURRIEDLY COMPLETED, FOR THE SAKE OF TIME, AN UNPALATABLE "AMUSE-BOUCHE" WILL RESULT THAT A WONDERFUL COMPLEMENTING WINE CANNOT SALVAGE.

I SINCERELY HOPE YOU HAVE FOUND A BENEFIT WHILE READING MY BOOK. IT IS MY DESIRE TO FURTHER SATANISM AS I TRULY BELIEVE IT WOULD MAKE OUR WORLD A BETTER PLACE IN WHICH TO LIVE. IF YOU ARE INTERESTED IN FURTHER ADVANCEMENT IN THE BLACK ARTS, FEEL FREE TO CONTACT ME.

I HAVE COUNSELED HUNDREDS OF THOSE SEEKERS WISHING TO FIND A SOLID FOOTING IN SATANISM. YOU SHOULD EXPECT TO INVEST IN SUCH PERSONALIZED GUIDANCE. EVERYONE NEEDS A HELPING HAND TO ACHIEVE THEIR GOALS AND ASK-

ING FOR HELP IS NOT A SIGN OF "WEAKNESS"; IT DEMONSTRATES INTELLIGENCE AND A SINCERE INTENTION TO TAKE THE SATANIC ARTS SERIOUSLY.

MAY THE BLESSINGS OF HELL POUR UPON YOU AND PROVIDE YOU WITH YOUR DESIRES. I WOULD LIKE TO HEAR FROM YOU. WRITE TO ME AT ALEISTERNACHT@ROCKETMAIL.COM OR VISIT MY WEBSITE AT WWW.ALEISTERNACHT.COM.

ALEISTER NACHT

GLOSSARY

ATHAME - A DOUBLE-EDGED RITUAL KNIFE USED IN MODERN WITCHCRAFT AND SATANISM.

AURIC - OF OR RELATING TO THE AURA SUPPOSEDLY SURROUNDING A LIVING CREATURE.

AUTO-DA-FÉ - THE RITUAL OF PUBLIC PENANCE OF CONDEMNED HERETICS AND APOSTATES.

BAPHOMET - BAPHOMET (/ˈBÆFƟMƐT/; FROM MEDIEVAL LATIN BAPHOMETH, BAFFOMETI, OCCITAN BAFOMETZ) IS AN IMAGINED PAGAN DEITY (I.E., A PRODUCT OF XTIAN FOLKLORE CONCERNING PAGANS), REVIVED IN THE 19TH CENTURY AS A FIGURE OF OCCULTISM AND SATANISM. IT FIRST APPEARED IN 11TH AND 12TH CENTURY LATIN AND PROVENÇAL AS A CORRUPTION OF "MAHOMET", THE LATINISATION OF "MUHAMMAD", BUT LATER

SANCTUM OF SHADOWS CORPUS SATANAS

IT APPEARED AS A TERM FOR A PAGAN IDOL IN TRIAL TRANSCRIPTS OF THE INQUISITION OF THE KNIGHTS TEMPLAR IN THE EARLY 14TH CENTURY. THE NAME FIRST CAME INTO POPULAR ENGLISH-SPEAKING CONSCIOUSNESS IN THE 19TH CENTURY, WITH DEBATE AND SPECULATION ON THE REASONS FOR THE SUPPRESSION OF THE TEMPLARS.

BLACK MAGIC - MAGIC INVOLVING THE SUPPOSED INVOCATION OF EVIL SPIRITS OR DEMONS FOR EVIL PURPOSES.

BLACK MASS - RITUAL OF THE CHURCH OF SATAN; PERFORMED TO BLASPHEME AND FREE THE PARTICIPANTS FROM THE HOLD OF ANYTHING WIDELY ACCEPTED AS SACRED, NOT JUST ORGANIZED RELIGION, AS IN THE TRADITIONAL BLACK MASS WHICH IS MEANT AS A BLASPHEMY AGAINST CATHOLICISM. (AKA MESSE NOIRE)

CAVEAT EMPTOR - THE PRINCIPLE THAT THE BUYER ALONE IS RESPONSIBLE FOR CHECKING THE QUALITY AND SUITABILITY OF GOODS BEFORE A PURCHASE IS MADE.

CHAKRA - CHAKRA ARE BELIEVED TO BE CENTERS OF THE BODY FROM WHICH A PERSON CAN COLLECT ENERGY. THEY ARE CONNECTED TO MAJOR ORGANS OR GLANDS THAT GOVERN OTHER BODY PARTS.

CHALICE - A CHALICE (FROM LATIN CALIX, CUP, BORROWED FROM GREEK KALYX, SHELL, HUSK) IS A GOBLET OR FOOTED CUP INTENDED TO HOLD A DRINK. IN GENERAL RELIGIOUS TERMS, IT IS INTENDED FOR DRINKING DURING A CEREMONY.

COITUS INTERRUPTUS - ALSO KNOWN AS THE REJECTED SEXUAL INTERCOURSE, WITHDRAWAL OR PULLOUT METHOD, IS A METHOD OF BIRTH-CON-

SANCTUM OF SHADOWS CORPUS SATANAS

TROL IN WHICH A MAN, DURING INTERCOURSE WITHDRAWS HIS PENIS FROM A WOMAN'S VAGINA PRIOR TO EJACULATION. THE MAN THEN DIRECTS HIS EJACULATE (SEMEN) AWAY FROM HIS PARTNER'S VAGINA TO AVOID INSEMINATION.

CONCUBINE - CONCUBINAGE IS AN INTERPER-SONAL RELATIONSHIP IN WHICH A PERSON ENGAGES IN AN ONGOING RELATIONSHIP (USUALLY MAT-RIMONIALLY ORIENTED) WITH ANOTHER PERSON TO WHOM THEY ARE NOT OR CANNOT BE MARRIED; THE INABILITY TO MARRY IS USUALLY DUE TO A DIFFERENCE IN SOCIAL STATUS OR ECONOMIC CON-DITION. HISTORICALLY, THE RELATIONSHIP IN-VOLVED A MAN IN A HIGHER STATUS POSITION, USUALLY WITH A LEGALLY SANCTIONED SPOUSE, WHO MAINTAINS A SECOND HOUSEHOLD WITH THE LESSER "SPOUSE". THE WOMAN IN SUCH A RELA-TIONSHIP IS REFERRED TO AS A CONCUBINE.

170

CONJURE - TO MAKE (SOMETHING) APPEAR UNEXPECTEDLY OR SEEMINGLY FROM NOWHERE AS BY MAGIC.

COVEN - A GROUP OR GATHERING OF WITCHES OR SATANISTS WHO MEET REGULARLY.

CRONE - HIGH RANKING MEMBER OF A SATANIC COVEN. ASSISTS AND ADVISES THE COVEN HIGH PRIESTESS ON MAGIC, RITUAL AND COVEN HISTORICAL ACCOUNTS.

DEMONOLOGY - THE STUDY OF DEMONS OR OF DEMONIC BELIEF.

DIVINE COMEDY - THE DIVINE COMEDY (ITALIAN: DIVINA COMMEDIA) IS AN EPIC POEM WRITTEN BY DANTE ALIGHIERI BETWEEN 1308 AND HIS DEATH IN 1321.

IT IS WIDELY CONSIDERED THE PREEMINENT WORK OF ITALIAN LITERATURE, AND IS SEEN AS

ONE OF THE GREATEST WORKS OF WORLD LITERA-
TURE. THE POEM'S IMAGINATIVE AND ALLEGORICAL
VISION OF THE AFTERLIFE IS A CULMINATION OF
THE MEDIEVAL WORLD-VIEW AS IT HAD DEVELOPED
IN THE WESTERN CHURCH. IT HELPED ESTABLISH THE
TUSCAN DIALECT, IN WHICH IT IS WRITTEN, AS THE
STANDARDIZED ITALIAN LANGUAGE. IT IS DIVIDED
INTO THREE PARTS: INFERNO, PURGATORIO, AND
PARADISO.

EVOCATION - THE ACT OF CALLING OR SUM-
MONING A SPIRIT, DEMON, GOD OR OTHER SUPER-
NATURAL AGENT, IN THE WESTERN MYSTERY TRA-
DITION. COMPARABLE PRACTICES EXIST IN MANY
RELIGIONS AND MAGICAL TRADITIONS AND MAY
USE POTIONS WITH AND WITHOUT UTTERED WORD
FORMULAS.

FASCHING - THE GERMAN CARNIVAL SEASON.

SANCTUM OF SHADOWS CORPUS SATANAS

GRIMOIRE - A GRIMOIRE IS A DESCRIPTION OF A SET OF MAGICAL SYMBOLS / ACTIONS AND HOW TO COMBINE THEM PROPERLY.

HABIT (CLOTH) - A LONG, LOOSE GARMENT WORN BY A MEMBER OF A RELIGIOUS ORDER OR CONGREGATION.

HELL - A PLACE REGARDED IN VARIOUS RELIGIONS AS A SPIRITUAL REALM OF EVIL AND SUFFERING, OFTEN TRADITIONALLY DEPICTED AS A PLACE OF PERPETUAL FIRE BENEATH THE EARTH WHERE THE WICKED ARE PUNISHED AFTER DEATH.

HIGHER MAGIC - HIGHER ORDER OF COGNITIVE AND MAGICAL ABILITIES.

INCANTATION - A SERIES OF WORDS SAID AS A MAGIC SPELL.

INCUBUS - A MALE DEMON THAT HAS SEXUAL INTERCOURSE WITH SLEEPING WOMEN.

INNER SANCTUM - THE MOST SACRED PLACE OF MAGICAL WORKINGS FOR A COVEN.

INVERTED PENTAGRAM - A FIVE-POINTED STAR THAT IS FORMED BY DRAWING A CONTINUOUS LINE IN FIVE STRAIGHT SEGMENTS, OFTEN USED AS A MYSTIC AND MAGICAL SYMBOL. OFTEN USED BY OCCULT PRACTITIONERS.

INVOCATION - THE ACTION OF INVOKING SOMETHING OR SOMEONE FOR ASSISTANCE OR AS AN AUTHORITY. AN INVOCATION (FROM THE LATIN VERB INVOCARE "TO CALL ON, INVOKE, TO GIVE") MAY TAKE THE FORM OF: SUPPLICATION, PRAYER OR SPELL. A FORM OF POSSESSION.

COMMAND OR CONJURATION.

SELF-IDENTIFICATION WITH CERTAIN SPIRITS.

LEX TALIONIS - LAW OF THE JUNGLE OR THE TALON. THE NATURAL ORDER WHERE THE WEAK ARE

ALLOWED TO PERISH, THE STRONG SURVIVE. DAR-
WIN'S SURVIVAL OF THE FITTEST.

LHP - LEFT-HAND PATH, IS A TERM USED IN
THE WESTERN ESOTERICISM.

LOUP-GAROU - A PERSON CURSED TO LIVE AS A
LYCANTHROPE. (AKA WEREWOLF).

MESSE NOIRE - SEE BLACK MASS.

NOSTRADAMUS - MICHEL DE NOSTREDAME,
USUALLY LATINISED AS NOSTRADAMUS, WAS A
FRENCH APOTHECARY AND REPUTED SEER WHO
PUBLISHED COLLECTIONS OF PROPHECIES THAT HAVE
SINCE BECOME FAMOUS WORLDWIDE. HE IS BEST
KNOWN FOR HIS BOOK "LES PROPHETIES" (THE
PROPHECIES), THE FIRST EDITION OF WHICH AP-
PEARED IN 1555. SINCE THE PUBLICATION OF THIS
BOOK, WHICH HAS RARELY BEEN OUT OF PRINT
SINCE HIS DEATH, NOSTRADAMUS HAS ATTRACTED A

FOLLOWING THAT, ALONG WITH MUCH OF THE POPULAR PRESS, CREDITS HIM WITH PREDICTING MANY MAJOR WORLD EVENTS.

ORGASM - A CLIMAX OF SEXUAL EXCITEMENT, CHARACTERIZED BY FEELINGS OF PLEASURE CENTERED IN THE GENITALS AND (IN MEN) EXPERIENCED AS AN ACCOMPANIMENT TO EJACULATION.

POSER - ANARCHISTS WHO HIDE BEHIND SATANISM TO SATISFY THEIR OWN DESTRUCTIVE DESIRES; NOT THOSE OF SATAN.

RITE - A RELIGIOUS OR OTHER SOLEMN CEREMONY OR ACT.

RITUALE ROMANUM - THE ROMAN RITUAL (LATIN: RITUALE ROMANUM) IS ONE OF THE OFFICIAL RITUAL WORKS OF THE ROMAN RITE OF THE CATHOLIC CHURCH. IT CONTAINS ALL THE SERVICES WHICH MAY BE PERFORMED BY A PRIEST OR DEA-

CON WHICH ARE NOT CONTAINED WITHIN EITHER THE MISSALE ROMANUM OR THE BREVARIUM ROMANUM. THE BOOK ALSO CONTAINS SOME OF THE RITES WHICH ARE CONTAINED IN ONLY ONE OF THESE BOOKS FOR CONVENIENCE.

SAMAEL - SAMAEL (HEBREW: סמאל) (ALSO SAMMAEL AND SAMIL) IS AN IMPORTANT ARCHANGEL IN TALMUDIC AND POST-TALMUDIC LORE, A FIGURE WHO IS ACCUSER, SEDUCER AND DESTROYER, AND HAS BEEN REGARDED AS BOTH GOOD AND EVIL.

SEX MAGIC - SEX MAGIC IS A TERM FOR VARIOUS TYPES OF SEXUAL ACTIVITY USED IN MAGICAL, RITUALISTIC, OR OTHERWISE RELIGIOUS AND SPIRITUAL PURSUITS. ONE PRACTICE OF SEX MAGIC IS USING THE ENERGY OF SEXUAL AROUSAL OR ORGASM WITH VISUALIZATION OF A DESIRED RESULT.

A PREMISE OF SEX MAGIC IS THE IDEA THAT SEXUAL ENERGY IS A POTENT FORCE THAT CAN BE HARNESSED TO TRANSCEND ONE'S NORMALLY PERCEIVED REALITY. ORAL, VAGINAL, ANAL AND OTHER METHODS ARE EMPLOYED DURING SEX MAGIC RITUALS.

SHEMHAMFORASH - THE SHEMHAMPHORASCH IS A CORRUPTION OF THE HEBREW TERM SHEM HA-MEPHORASH (שם המפורש), WHICH WAS USED IN TANNAITIC TIMES TO REFER TO THE TETRAGRAMMATON. IN EARLY KABBALAH THE TERM WAS USED TO DESIGNATE SOMETIMES A SEVENTY-TWO LETTER NAME FOR GOD, AND SOMETIMES A FORTY-TWO LETTER NAME. RASHI SAID SHEM HA-MEPHORASH WAS USED FOR A FORTY-TWO LETTER NAME, BUT MAIMONIDES THOUGHT SHEM HA-MEPHORASH WAS USED ONLY FOR THE FOUR LETTER TETRAGRAMMATON.

SIGIL OF BAPHOMET - THE SEAL OR IMAGE OF BAPHOMET. ALSO SEE BAPHOMET.

SOCRATIC METHOD - THE SOCRATIC METHOD (ALSO KNOWN AS METHOD OF ELENCHUS, ELENCTIC METHOD, SOCRATIC IRONY, OR SOCRATIC DEBATE), NAMED AFTER THE CLASSICAL GREEK PHILOSOPHER SOCRATES, IS A FORM OF INQUIRY AND DEBATE BETWEEN INDIVIDUALS WITH OPPOSING VIEWPOINTS BASED ON ASKING AND ANSWERING QUESTIONS TO STIMULATE CRITICAL THINKING AND TO ILLUMINATE IDEAS. IT IS A DIALECTICAL METHOD, OFTEN INVOLVING AN OPPOSITIONAL DISCUSSION IN WHICH THE DEFENSE OF ONE POINT OF VIEW IS PITTED AGAINST THE DEFENSE OF ANOTHER; ONE PARTICIPANT MAY LEAD ANOTHER TO CONTRADICT HIMSELF IN SOME WAY, THUS STRENGTHENING THE INQUIRER'S OWN POINT.

SUCCUBUS - A FEMALE DEMON BELIEVED TO

HAVE SEXUAL INTERCOURSE WITH SLEEPING MEN.

SATANIC BIBLE - THE SATANIC BIBLE IS A COL-
LECTION OF ESSAYS, OBSERVATIONS, AND RITUALS
PUBLISHED BY ANTON LAVEY IN 1969. IT CON-
TAINS THE CORE PRINCIPLES OF THE RELIGION OF
LAVEYAN SATANISM, AND IS CONSIDERED THE
FOUNDATION OF ITS PHILOSOPHY AND DOGMA. IT
HAS BEEN DESCRIBED AS THE MOST IMPORTANT
DOCUMENT TO INFLUENCE CONTEMPORARY
LAVEYAN SATANISM. THOUGH THE SATANIC
BIBLE IS NOT CONSIDERED TO BE SACRED SCRIPTURE
IN THE WAY THE XTIAN BIBLE IS TO XTIANITY,
LAVEYAN SATANISTS REGARD IT AS AN AUTHORI-
TATIVE TEXT; IT HAS BEEN REFERRED TO AS "QUASI-
SCRIPTURE." IT EXTOLS THE VIRTUES OF EXPLORING
ONE'S OWN NATURE AND INSTINCTS. BELIEVERS
HAVE BEEN DESCRIBED AS "ATHEISTIC SATANISTS" BE-
CAUSE THEY BELIEVE THAT GOD IS NOT AN EXTER-

NAL ENTITY, BUT RATHER SOMETHING THAT EACH PERSON CREATES AS A PROJECTION OF HIS OR HER OWN PERSONALITY—A BENEVOLENT AND STABILIZING FORCE IN HIS OR HER LIFE. AT THE TIME OF PRINTING OF SANCTUM OF SHADOWS, THERE HAVE BEEN THIRTY PRINTINGS OF THE SATANIC BIBLE, THROUGH WHICH IT HAS SOLD OVER A MILLION COPIES.

SWOT ANALYSIS - A USEFUL TECHNIQUE FOR UNDERSTANDING YOUR STRENGTHS AND WEAKNESSES, AND FOR IDENTIFYING BOTH THE OPPORTUNITIES OPEN TO YOU AND THE THREATS YOU FACE.

THIRD EYE - THE INNATE ABILITY TO SENSE AND UNDERSTAND MORE THAN MEETS THE EYE.

THURIBLE - A THURIBLE IS A METAL CENSER SUSPENDED FROM CHAINS, IN WHICH INCENSE IS

BURNED DURING WORSHIP SERVICES.

THURIFER - THE PERSON WHO CARRIES THE THURIBLE.

VAMPIRE - THOSE BEINGS (UNDEAD OR LIVING CREATURE) WHO SURVIVE BY FEEDING ON THE BLOOD OF LIVING CREATURES.

WIMPLE - A CLOTH HEADDRESS COVERING THE HEAD, THE NECK, AND THE SIDES OF THE FACE, FORMERLY WORN BY WOMEN AND STILL WORN BY SOME NUNS.

EPILOGUS

" 'A VOWES BY PAPER, PEN AND INKE,

AND BY THE LEARNED SISTERS' DRINKE,

TO SPEND HIS TIME, HIS LAMPS, HIS OYLE,

AND NEVER CEASE HIS BRAINE TO TOYLE,

TILL FROM THE SILENT HOURES OF NIGHT

HEE DOTH PRODUCE FOR YOUR DELIGHT,

CONCEITS SO NEW, SO HARMLESS FREE,

THAT PURITANS THEM-SELVES MAY SEE

A PLAY......."[17]

MY LITERARY CONUNDRUM CAME TO FRUITION SHORTLY AFTER MY FIRST BOOK WAS PUBLISHED. LIKE SO MANY AUTHORS, I FOUND MYSELF AT A "CAREER CROSSROAD"; "WHERE DO I GO FROM HERE?" THE THOUGHT OF THIS, EVEN YEARS LATER, CAUSES A CHILL TO RUN UP MY SPINE.

THE QUESTION WAS "WOULD I ALIENATE MY NEWLY-FOUND READERS BY REVEALING MY TRUE NATURE, BELIEFS AND EXPERIENCES OR DO I FORGE

---

[17] *Epilogue of "Ram-Alley or Merry Tricks"* by Lording Barry (1611)

MY WAY INTO THE LITERARY MAINSTREAM?" JUST LIKE OTHERS IN MY LITERARY CAMP, I HAD WORKED SO DILIGENTLY FOR SO LONG; WAS I PREPARED TO THROW THAT AWAY? PERSONAL INTEGRITY COMES WITH A PRICE. VERY FEW ASPIRING AUTHORS EARN ENOUGH ROYALTIES TO SURVIVE MUCHNESS THRIVE; IF AN AUTHOR IS SUCCESSFUL IN ANY CAPACITY, IT IS AKIN TO WINNING THE LOTTERY. DOES SOMEONE JUST WALK AWAY FROM THAT GOOD FORTUNE?

TO BE HUMAN IS SOMETIMES VERY, VERY COSTLY AND NOT JUST FOR ME. THERE WERE THOSE WHO WERE COUNTING ON MY NEXT BOOK TO BE A "WINNER". MANY PEOPLE DEPEND ON MY BOOKS TO SELL; IT IS A SINGLE LITERARY / FISCAL MICROCOSM; A RESPONSIBILITY NEITHER FULLY APPRECIATED NOR WANTED. WAS I TO FADE INTO OBSCURITY WITH MILLIONS OF OTHER ASPIRING, UNDEREMPLOYED WRITERS?

BEING A BEST-SELLING, SUCCESSFUL AUTHOR IS LIKE SCREWING WITHOUT A PROPHYLACTIC; IT FEELS GREAT BUT IT CAN HAVE FAR-REACHING RAMIFICATIONS. IN THE BROADER SENSE, I WENT RUBBER-LESS INTO EVERY ORIFICE. WITH THE RE-

LEASE OF THE NEXT BOOK, SWEET SUCCESS FELT MORE LIKE "BUYER'S REMORSE".

AS I BEGAN READING ONE OF THE NEGATIVE REVIEWS OF MY WORK, "BOOK OF SATANIC MAGIC", MY FIRST INSTINCT WAS TO SEND THE REVIEWERS A GAGGLE OF DEMONS WITH "INCURABLE ASS ITCH"!! I AM HUMAN AND WHILE I STRIVE TO BE OBJECTIVE, CALLING ONE OF MY "LITERARY BABIES" UGLY IN A PUBLIC FORUM, WAS A BIT "STINGING" TO SAY THE LEAST!

A CALMER HEAD PREVAILED AND AFTER A 'COOLING-OFF PERIOD', I BEGAN TO UNDERSTAND THE REVIEWER'S POINT OF VIEW. THIS WAS NOT A PERSONAL ATTACK; FAR FROM IT. THIS WAS A VALID CONTRAST OF THE OLD, TIRED, ATHEISTIC "LAVEYANISM" AND MY NEWLY-DISCOVERED EMBARKATION ON A JOURNEY OF DOCUMENTING MY EXPERIENCES AS A TRUE DEVIL WORSHIPER.

I BEGAN WRITING AND CONSISTENTLY CHOKING DOWN ANY RESEMBLANCE OF COMMERCIAL-SUCCESS MOTIVATIONS OR ASPIRATIONS. THESE WERE MY BELIEFS, MY EXPERIENCES, MY PROCESSES AND "MY STORY" AS OPPOSED TO REBRANDING OF YESTERDAY'S STALE SATANIC BELIEFS. I HAVE NEVER

BEEN AN ATHEIST; THAT WOULD MAKE ME A TOTAL HYPOCRITE. I HAVE EXPERIENCED AND INTERACTED WITH SATAN AND DEMONS FOR OVER TWENTY-FIVE YEARS AND COUNTING!! I WAS WALKING A TIGHTROPE; WOULD ANYONE FIND VALUE IN MY WORDS OR WAS THIS "SUCCESS" SIMPLY A DREAM?

SINCE COMPLETING THE FIRST IN THE "SANC-TUM OF SHADOWS" SERIES, I HAVE RECEIVED OVERWHELMING APPROVAL FROM READERS. THIS SEEMS TO INDICATE A "MORE INTELLECTUAL" READ-ERSHIP WHICH APPLAUDS MATURATION OF THOSE WILLING TO EXPLORE ADVANCED TECHNIQUES AND PROCESSES.

THERE MUST BE A POSITIVE, REWARDING REC-IPROCITY BETWEEN AUTHOR AND READER. IF NOT, THE AUTHOR CEASES TO PRODUCE OR THE READER LOOSES INTEREST. THERE IS NEITHER A SHORTAGE OF AUTHORS NOR READERS TO FILL THE VOID.

WE LIVE IN A WONDERFUL TIME IN HISTORY WHEN AN OBSCURE AUTHOR, AS MYSELF, IS ABLE TO ATTRACT A RECEPTIVE AUDIENCE OF INTELLI-GENT, RESPONSIBLE, DISCERNING AND ARTICULATE READERS. BRAVO!!

AUTHORS MUST GROW, DEVELOP AND EVOLVE;

WE ALL DO THIS IN SOME CAPACITY THROUGHOUT OUR INDIVIDUAL LIVES. OUR COLLECTIVE ABILITIES TO REASON WHAT WE HEAR AND READ, SEPARATES HUMANS FROM OUR NOT-SO-DISTANT COUSINS IN THE ANIMAL KINGDOM.

I ENJOY SHARING MY EXPERIENCES AND THOUGHTS WITH AN ACCEPTING AUDIENCE AND I CHERISH THE OPPORTUNITIES TO ENLIGHTEN THOSE SEARCHING FOR A BEDROCK FOUNDATION ON WHICH TO BUILD HIS / HER BELIEFS AND LIFE-LONG JOURNEY.

WE ARE "LOGICIANS" BY MERE VIRTUE AND WE INSTINCTIVELY SEEK TO SOLVE A RIDDLE OR UNDERSTAND THE INNER WORKINGS OF ANY PROCESS. WE ARE CHALLENGED BY WHAT IS JUST BEYOND THE HORIZON AND WE INTRINSICALLY RESEARCH, LEARN, HYPOTHESIZE AND PROVE / DISPROVE OUR ASSUMPTIONS. WE ARE SO SIMILAR IN CONSTRUCTION YET DISSIMILAR IN INDIVIDUAL APPROACHES.

ONLY YOU KNOW WHAT IS IN YOUR HEART. AS YOU STAND AT THE EDGE OF THE DARK ABYSS AND LOOK OVER THE EDGE, ONLY YOU KNOW YOUR MOTIVES, YOUR MOTIVATIONS, YOUR PLEASURES AND YOUR TREASURES OF WHICH YOU ARE SEARCH-

ING TO FIND.

DO NOT LIMIT YOURSELF IN SCOPE FOR IF YOU HAVE READ THIS BOOK SIMPLY TO CONJURE A DEMON, YOU NEED NOT LOOK VERY FAR. THERE ARE DEMONS ON EVERY STREET CORNER AROUND THE WORLD. IF YOU HOWEVER, ARE SEEKING TO ENLIGHTEN YOURSELF, MEDITATE ON MY WORDS AND BROADEN YOUR PERSPECTIVES. DO NOT LOOK WITH BLINDERS ANY LONGER FOR THERE ARE THOSE ORGANIZATIONS WHO COLLECTIVELY SEEK TO ENSLAVE THE INTELLIGENT AND PASSIONATE. YOU MUST DECIDE IF THE COGNITIVE BATTLE WILL BE DECIDED IN YOUR FAVOR.

DO NOT GO FREELY INTO INVOLUNTARY SERVITUDE, FOR THOSE WHO SPEAK IN THE "AUTHORITY-AFFIRMATIVE" ONLY FOOL THEMSELVES. LISTEN TO THOSE WHO WILL SAY "I KNOW THERE IS SOMETHING GREATER." WITHOUT THOSE WHO REMIND US OF DOUBT, REASONING WILL SURELY CEASE TO EXIST.

SATANISM, DEMONOLOGY, WITCHCRAFT, BLACK MAGIC, DEVIL WORSHIP; NAMES CREATED BY HUMANS TO EXPLAIN THE "UNEXPLAINABLE" AND IN SOME CASES, THE INCOMPREHENSIBLE. I

CONTINUE TO WRITE ABOUT SUCH MATTERS AND OFTEN FIND MYSELF PRESSING THE 'DELETE' KEY; I SIMPLY TALK MYSELF OUT OF WHAT I HAVE WRITTEN BECAUSE IT SOUNDS TOO FAR-FETCHED......TOTALLY UNBELIEVABLE. PERHAPS THIS IS BECAUSE REASONING TAKES PRECEDENT OVER THE BELIEF IN MAGIC ITSELF.

SOCIETY RELENTLESSLY SEARCHES FOR ANY PLAUSIBLE JUSTIFICATION; LOGICAL EXPLANATIONS FOR THAT WHICH CANNOT BE REDUCED TO OUR SIMPLISTIC, HUMANISTIC UNDERSTANDING OF THE UNIVERSE SURROUNDING US. IF WE CANNOT EXPLAIN SOMETHING, DOES IT CEASE TO EXIST? OF COURSE NOT!

I LOOK FORWARD TO THE FUTURE AND IF THE FIRST SANCTUM OF SHADOWS INSTALLMENT IS ANY INDICATION OF THINGS TO COME, I BELIEVE MY READERS ARE LOOKING FORWARD TO OUR FUTURE TOGETHER ALSO.

ALEISTER NACHT

ECCE HOMO

AUTHOR ALEISTER NACHT IS A SATANIC MAGUS AND LEADER OF A NATIONAL SATANIC COVEN COMPRISING OF NUMEROUS GROUPS LOCATED IN FLORIDA, LOUISIANA AND OKLAHOMA.

WITH A MODERN VIEW OF SATANISM, HE BRINGS THE DARKNESS TO LIFE IN A VERY TANGIBLE MANNER. HIS BOOKS HAVE FOUND FAVOR WITH A MULTITUDE OF SEARCHERS CROSSING ALL DEMOGRAPHIC AND WORLD-WIDE GEOGRAPHIC BOUNDARIES.

ALEISTER NACHT'S DIGITAL AND HARD-COPY BOOKS ARE DISTRIBUTED WORLD-WIDE BY LOKI / SPECKBOHNE PUBLISHING.

ALEISTER NACHT LIVES IN THE TAMPA BAY AREA AND ENJOYS THE "SALT LIFE".

YOU CAN FIND MORE INFORMATION ABOUT
ALEISTER NACHT ON HIS WEBSITE.
WWW.ALEISTERNACHT.COM

ALEISTER NACHT'S SATANIC MAGIC BLOG
CONTAINS A WEALTH OF INFORMATION ABOUT
SATANISM AND DEVIL WORSHIP.
WWW.SATANICMAGIC.WORDPRESS.COM

THE COVEN IS A SUBSCRIPTION-BASED WEBSITE
WHERE FUTURE SATANISTS LEARN THE OPERATIONS
OF SATANIC MAGIC AND COVEN MANAGEMENT.
WWW.ALEISTERNACHT.PODBEAN.COM

Made in the USA
Middletown, DE
13 October 2024

62529075R00108